The Modern Pioneer's Guide

The Modern Pioneer's Guide

Shelf Stable Stovetop Recipes, Herbal Remedies,
72 Hour Kit Planning & Long Term Camping Tips

BY ASHLEY PARKINSON

spring creek
BOOK COMPANY
Provo, Utah

ISBN: 978-0-9960974-7-5
e. 1

Published by:
Spring Creek Book Company

www.springcreekbooks.com

Cover design © Spring Creek Book Company
Cover image © Sheri Hoth
Editor: Stephanie Hall

Printed in the United States of America
Printed on acid-free paper

Dedication

This book is dedicated to all my family, friends, and anyone who is looking for another resource to be better prepared! I wanted to take this opportunity to publicly give a special thank you to my sweet friends who have been such a huge part of this creation.

A sincere thank you to Tiffany Vail, my precious sister. Words cannot express my love and admiration for the exemplary character and righteous example you have always been to me. Your loyalty, integrity, and your kind heart are unsurpassed by anyone I know. I am so grateful that I was given such a perfect sister and best friend.

Stephanie Hall, "my adopted sister," tireless editor, and longtime best friend. It's not every day you find a kindred spirit who you connect with immediately and stay close to for the rest of your life . . . I am so grateful that I found you. It's now more than 15 years later and we still talk every day, I love that! You're such an amazing example of friendship and love.

Renee Parkinson, my amazing mother-in-law who has been with me through everything all these years and is one of my dearest best friends. What an outstanding woman of devotion, strength, and love you are. I am so amazed at all the service you are continually doing for others. How grateful I am for our wonderful relationship we've had all these years.

Suzanne Newson, my steadfast sounding board. I love how we've been so connected over the years. Those fun college days when we had our small families together seem like yesterday. I am so grateful that we have each other to chat with. You're such a beautiful example of motherhood, patience, and love. I'm so grateful to have you as a best friend in my life. I cherish our friendship so much!

Renae Kingsley, my motivational and treasured best friend who is such an inspiration to me. Watching you devote your life to the Lord and your children always encourages me to strive to be my very best! You're friendship is such a special gift in my life and I am so appreciative to know you and to talk as often as we do!

You ladies have all listened to my endless chatter about food storage for years, tried recipes I've asked you to try, and always been such a wonderful support to me through my journey with this project, as well as many others I've embarked on throughout the years. You have all stood by me for decades. How blessed I have been to have such true and loving relationships. You have all been my closest friends for at least 10 years, and many of you longer than that! You make my days shiny and bright every time I get to talk with you. I wouldn't be who I am without all of you. Thank you all so much. I am so grateful to have such extraordinary best friends in my life!

My deepest gratitude to my wonderful family for all the taste-testing and great suggestions. I have so much admiration for my sweet husband. You're my very best friend and I love sharing life with you. You have always supported my ideas and given me such strength. No one will ever be more grateful to you than I am for all the dishes you helped wash and the amazing re-seasoning you did for my cast iron. You put so much time and love into helping me any way you could . . . how blessed I am to have you. And what troopers my little girls have been with every meal I put in front of them! They would give me the thumbs up to put a recipe in the book, or tell me what the dish needed in order to be better. They are my true motivation to have a functioning food storage. I adore my family and truly love nourishing them and teaching my daughters about the principles of provident living. I am so grateful to my family for being excited about incorporating food storage meals and for being so supportive.

I feel a very deep gratitude as well to my loving Heavenly Father. My love and respect for Him go beyond what I could put into words. I love being a member of the Church of Jesus Christ of Latter-day Saints. It has greatly influenced my life, as well as this book. Our Heavenly Father has given all of us such wonderful insight, diligent warning, and tender guidance to all His children that will listen and who strive to follow the wise council from His prophets and apostles. I am so grateful for the resources of the LDS Church, talks by LDS Church leaders, and wonderful testimonies that many have shared about being prepared.

Ashley Parkinson

Contents

Chapter 8: Suppers

Soups, Chowder & Stews

Meals

Chapter 9: Desserts

Chapter 1

Why I Created This Book

It was October of 2011, and the weather in upstate New York at that time of year is always crisp and delicious. There were golden leaves in a variety of shades dressing the trees and just a few had started to fall to the ground. The weather was still pleasant and my house was buzzing with excitement. We had my husband's sister over for the week to visit. It was a big deal for my little ones because their aunt lived in Idaho and they didn't get to see her too often.

The house was full of chatter, games, yummy food and plenty of people. We had just gotten news of the forecast for an unpredicted early snow storm that was going to hit. We were used to heavy snows in the northeast, but not this early in the year. The weather had been so unseasonably warm the past few years that it wasn't common to start seeing snow until the late part of November.

My husband had taken some time off work while his sister was in town. We had just taken her to New York City and showed her the sights the day before. The next day, it was snowing and the flakes were heavy and wet. The trees were being outlined in thick white snow and the leaves on them looked like clusters of white clouds. Everything was so pretty, but so cold!

I started to do my laundry. I had a few loads that I had let build up. We were having so much fun with my husband's sister that I was putting the household chores off as long as I could while she was in town. I started the dishwasher and had just put some homemade bread in the oven. The house was smelling good, the appliances were clinking and humming, letting me know they were all on task and doing their jobs, and the kids were all prepared to take showers and get ready for an early bedtime after we had dinner.

Out of nowhere, the power went out. In the middle of all my preparing . . . it was gone! The power had crashed for massive areas all over in update New York. The trees were so heavy with all the wet snow that they were falling over onto power lines and transformers, knocking out power in many cities. The amount of affected people was huge. Where we lived was a small hamlet (which is even smaller than a village). National Grid's focus was to repair the larger cities first, then work their way out to the smaller surrounding areas. Stores, gas stations, and more were shut down. We were in a real life natural disaster!

Power outages are pretty frequent in New York during the winter time, but like I mentioned, this was not winter time and it was really unexpected. They usually only last for a few hours, or a day or two at the most. I felt completely taken by surprise, especially since I was preparing amidst the coming storm. The bread stopped baking, the appliances paused mid-cycle, and all the kids were upset. What had happened?!?

I had become interested in being prepared and having food storage when we started having children. What we had stored certainly wasn't enough to feed us for a long period of time. It seemed that everything that could have gone wrong did that week. We had no paper plates or supplies, and all our dishes were dirty. There was hardly any water to wash anything, let alone flush the toilets. Our neighbor had a generator, but it broke. We had no clothes because they were all dirty and in the middle of getting washed!

I tried making meager meals with the food we had. We even melted snow for water. We had a small camping cook stove and it took forever, and used a lot of propane. Plus it was freezing outside and the wind was so strong, that even going outside to cook was a hazard. What was worse was the cold. There was no heat and my husband's sister was getting a horrible cough!

We stayed without power for two nights at our home. We all looked so pathetic, tired, hungry, and dirty. My little ones ended up snuggling with their aunt to try and keep warm at night. We eventually had to call surrender and went to a larger city that was a long drive away to stay in one of the hotels that still had power. There were a few businesses there that had power, Barnes and Nobel being one of them. So we would hang out there and read books with the kids all day and then go back to the hotel that evening. Soon it was time to take my sister-in-law to the airport. She was more than anxious to get back to the 21st century, and I couldn't blame her. The day after she left, the power came back on in our area. So all in all, we were without power for almost an entire week.

I was amazed at how fragile we all really are. I had food, but no heat, not near enough water, and our home wasn't prepared in a way to invite a calmness to the situation, either. We had flashlights and batteries, but we really didn't have much that helped us through this ordeal.

To say it shook my confidence in my preparedness efforts was an understatement. To this day, if I even hear so much of a whisper about a rain storm, I make sure the house is totally clean and dinner is ready in advance. Storms and natural disasters scare me. It's horrible to not be prepared, but it's even worse when you are trying to prepare and the storm is already upon you!

So why did I write this book? One of the things that I have really become passionate about is being prepared (shocker, I know). Food storage is something in particular that I absolutely just love to talk about. Not the idea of obtaining food and storing it, but about having a truly functional food storage that you can use. One that tastes good, too. I personally wanted food storage meals that I could serve to friends and not cringe, dishes that my family would enjoy, while at the same time being easy, healthy, and fast.

It was such a battle finding anything that tasted good and was actually shelf stable. Some recipes called for freeze dried foods... they are expensive. I wanted to find something really affordable. Other recipes used ovens! Even if I wanted to use a sun oven, I live in New York. We only get sun for about 2 months out of the year. The rest of the year, it is either raining or snowing. I have a sun oven and can hardly even think about using it, so stovetop was definitely the way I wanted to go.

I wanted stovetop recipes that I could cook over a fire outside, on our wood burning stove, or even on a butane stove right in my home. Some recipes would use partly shelf stable ingredients and then call for perishable items like cheese or dairy. I also wanted something that used canned ingredients so I didn't have to pre-make anything. It needed to be quick and easy with little prep work involved. I also found recipes that used a lot of processed foods. I am not a food snob, but I didn't want cheese-wiz in my pantry. I wanted whole foods, something that used plenty of whole grains, vegetables, beans, and legumes. Many recipes had nearly no spices or flavor in them. They tasted bland and my family wouldn't eat them...I will be honest, I didn't want to either!

I looked high and low for a cookbook that used shelf stable ingredients, something without any freeze dried foods. I wanted a book that made meals which were completely stovetop based, that also tasted delicious. I couldn't find it anywhere.

I didn't just want a food storage that was a mix of random ingredients. I wanted something that I could make meals out of that correlated to recipes. I wanted to start eating the recipes now and incorporate them into our weekly meal planning. I really wanted to get my own food storage organized.

I started creating meals that met all my requirements. I made spice blends so they tasted delicious and took them from drab to fab. I got creative and found recipes that used the stovetop and then tweaked them to be shelf stable and improve them in any way I needed to. I prayed, oh did I pray! I wanted breakfasts, breads, soups, meals, and desserts! I wanted variety and foods from all over the globe that we enjoy eating on a regular basis in our home.

As I started writing all my recipes down, I had the distinct impression to share this with others. Other people would love to be able to cook like this and have it in their preparedness kits. These recipes are things that can feed a lot of people easily, be useful for long term camping, and help so many more people than just the ones in my home.

Writing a cookbook wasn't on my radar. I was in graduate school getting my master's degree. I was juggling work with my home commitments, and I was busy. I couldn't shake the feeling though, and all the excitement in me to actually tackle this idea of writing a book just wouldn't leave my mind. I would go to sleep thinking about it and I would get up thinking about it. I was nervous . . . maybe there wasn't a book like this out there because it couldn't be done? I prayed, wanting to know that my Heavenly Father was going to help me with this project that I felt He wanted me to do.

As always, He helped. I had amazing amounts of inspiration throughout this entire process. Whenever I would get nervous about tackling a new thing in the book, like stovetop biscuits for example, a calm peace would just come over me. My worries would fade, and the right ideas and techniques would enter my mind. A way to make everything I really wanted to have in this book was truly provided.

My family has some very amazing women who were legend for their cooking skills. My grandmother RaNae Foster, her sister Ilene Sherman, and their mother Carrol Waddell (my great grandmother) have all created masterpieces in the kitchen. I felt so much support from these amazing women when making this book. I would pause and ask myself what would they do, what would they tweak, would this meet their standard of deliciousness? I am so grateful for the amazing example they showed me about how to cook with real love, commitment, and care. I still fondly remember both my grandmother and my great grandmother fussing over the stove and the oven, constantly checking, smelling, and watching their mouth-watering morsels cook to perfection.

I have always loved cooking, and cooking from scratch. If I got to pick a show to watch on the television, it would always be a cooking show. I loved watching Julia Child's program and the Food Network. I read cookbooks like others read novels. I still love pouring over the stories, techniques, and recipes in them. I have always enjoyed making yummy food. I wanted this book to have that element of me in it. I saw myself checking, smelling, taste testing, tweaking and fussing over all these dishes with the same anxious excitement of my grandmothers. I was eager to create something outstanding. I was channeling all the wonderful cooking from my family into this book.

This cookbook, aside from having its unique strategy for making meals, has a few untraditional additions to it as well. I have included some cleaning recipes, herbal remedies, and emergency planning ideas. I love making my own cleaning supplies and herbal remedies for our family, as well as planning out my family's emergency preps. I am excited to share with you some things that are a part of my home and bring it into yours.

I have trained as an herbalist for years. I wanted to glean anything I thought would be easy and helpful into this book. I included some treasured remedies that I have made and shared with friends as they came to visit over the years. I was so excited to be able to pass on some of the great and very useful information that I had learned into this book. I really believe that herbal remedies have a very practical place in the planning of your food storage. I was delighted to see the herbal remedies chapter unfold and to have the opportunity to share some of my favorite creations with you!

Though the focus is obtaining a food storage for emergency preparedness, this guide is really about so much more. Included in this book are ideas for preparing a 72 Hour Kit, some long term camping ideas, and also detailed lists of items recommended for any calamity that may come your way. All of these ideas can help you on your path to being better prepared. This book is not an all-inclusive guide, so keep adding to it and thinking of more ideas of what your family needs. You'll be amazed at the peace, clarity of mind, and the inspiration that will come as you try to be better prepared through following the principles of obedience rather than being chased by panic and fear.

This really is my food storage cookbook and emergency planning all wrapped into one guide. These are my family's go-to recipes for everything we need. From crepes to biscuits, from enchiladas to cobblers, it's all in this book! It also includes my family's lists of ideas for what we want to have in our emergency preparedness. I've added some encouraging and inspirational words from LDS Church leaders and scriptures to support us along the way.

These recipes are also ideal for emergency situations, such as natural disasters, financial emergencies, and mini emergencies (like not having anything planned for dinner, no one's made it to the grocery store yet, and so on). Because every single recipe uses shelf stable ingredients, they are ideal for college students, missionaries, newlyweds, young adults, and anyone who is looking for quick, healthy, and easy pantry cooking.

This guide is a wonderful addition to any emergency preparedness plan, as well as a beautiful gift to give someone learning how to cook simple and quick pantry meals on their own. I hope it touches you and inspires you to get creative with what you want to have in your food storage. I want this book to give you peace of mind, knowing there's always something in the pantry you can whip up on those nights that are unplanned and you get asked the question, "what's for dinner?" This was a project that completely enveloped me and was a joy to create. This book is truly a gift from my Heavenly Father to my family and to yours. Enjoy!

Chapter 2

Why This Book Is
So Different

This book is refreshingly different from other food storage cookbooks and preparedness guides! My recipes rely heavily on whole food, unprocessed, non-freeze dried ingredients, and they contain no eggs, butters, or other perishable ingredients. Plus I use a stovetop for ALL the recipes! There is no oven required. It's not only practical for planning shelf stable meals, but it's also a great resource for camping recipes, off-the-grid cooking, and self-reliant skills that can be made in all seasons. Another feature of this book is that I included 72 Hour Kit and long term camping ideas. These suggested items are ideal to reference when you are planning out your family's preparations.

I wanted to make this book for a few reasons. Most of the food storage based cookbooks I have tried before had shelf stable recipes that didn't really taste great. I'd try to coax my family into enjoying all the meals we tasted, but they were right—they didn't taste good. We would end up with leftovers no one wanted and scrambling for a new recipe that we hoped would taste better. The other thing that I was really looking for in a food storage cookbook was one that didn't use an oven. I wanted all the recipes to be stovetop based. Ones that could be made safely indoors with a butane stove, with a wood burning stove, or over an open fire. Having an oven (solar or not) wasn't something I wanted to rely on, in case bad weather didn't permit the use of one.

I've come across numerous half-fresh and half-canned recipes. I wanted the recipes that utilized our food storage to be 100% shelf stable. I avoided anything powdered or freeze dried (that requires rehydration) because it takes up so much valuable water to cook with those ingredients, not to mention being more expensive.

Only a handful of cookbooks that focused on food storage had anything about herbal remedies in them. Many used tinctures (which contain alcohol), and I was looking for recipes that were completely alcohol-free. No one had the simple basic recipes that you could use for everyday ailments. They focused more on using herbs for survival. I was looking for herbal cough syrups, teas, and oils. These are the items we use on a regular basis in my home.

I also saw how many people were stuck planning out their 72 Hour Kits and their other preparations. I wanted to break down all the categories so it was easier to plan out. I also wanted to give ideas, not strict rules of all the do's and don'ts. I think it's a personal and very individual choice when planning out what each family needs. I wanted to give a platform of ideas that anyone could take and build from, without feeling like they had to get everything I listed (as I've seen other sources do). This book was a wonderful opportunity to share with others what I have been able to present in workshops and other functions. These ideas have helped out so many families to see the options they have when planning out their family's preparations, and I really wanted to include that in this book.

When I started to plan out what we wanted to have in our food storage, I knew I needed to get organized, there were a lot of topics that I strongly felt I needed to include. So many people I talked to had massive amounts of basic ingredients, but no recipes or real plans on how to get the flour, oil, and salt to mix together and make a great meal. Most of the people I peppered for questions just said they would throw it all together and figure it out when they needed to. That idea scared me and wasn't a practical way to really rotate your food storage. I wanted to "store what we eat and eat what we store." Thus began the planning of what recipes we were going to make for our family's food storage.

The thought of helping others plan affordable, shelf stable meals and family preparations was so exciting! It motivated me to work on this project every spare minute of my day. I've been passionate about food storage for years, but never really figured out how to make it function until now. This book became the perfect answer.

As your family starts to make these recipes, find what works for you. Add more spice, double the recipes or reduce them, take out or add in something, tweak them to be whatever your family enjoys. These recipes are a great guide to help you plan out your meals. This book is also great to cook out of all year long and to enjoy together right now. Eating whole grains, adding more beans and legumes to your meals, and cooking over a stovetop more often will benefit you immensely. Start actually living off the foods that you're storing today!

The preparedness aspect of this book is meant to be just that, a guide. The items listed are meant to help you brainstorm and springboard off of when planning out your family's needs. This is not a source that will include everything you could possibly want to have when planning out your preparations. The ideas are a wonderful tool that can help you create the perfect custom plan for your specific family's needs! Take time to read over all the information and carefully consider what you should include in your kits and preps. This guide is a wonderful tool to get you on your way!

It's truly not every day that you come across a book that includes recipes that are: practical to prepare and taste delicious, includes herbal remedies that are simple to make and effective, with lots of ideas to help you plan out your 72 Hour Kits, and also list a slew of long-term camping items to consider when planning your preparations, without using fear and anxiety as it's motivation!

A Few Notes About
The Recipes

I didn't want to include a list of how much of each ingredient you should purchase. I did this for two main reasons. First, only you can know how much your family consumes, and you will know that better than any data recommendation from the Internet or books. Second, I wanted you to really try these recipes and see for yourself how much of something you will need, and if anything needs to be tweaked for your family's preferences. These recipes aren't meant to be a list of something you stockpile and wait to use. They're meant to be rotated through your family's meals right now.

I'm not just storing enough food to make these recipes, then calling my planning and provisions good. I am constantly adding any extra foods that I can: grains, beans, legumes, baking ingredients, extra canned items (whole foods, meats, soups, stews, etc.), additional water, and much more. I am also continually adding new recipes to my collection and finding more resources to create shelf stable meals.

Anything over the required amounts for these recipes is so important to have. The food we have on hand may help others who are desperately in need. Additional foods that we store may help your family if for some reason the foods or amounts you put aside are no longer adequate. It's something you honestly can never have too much of during times of need.

Being a member of The Church of Jesus Christ of Latter-day Saints (LDS), I will be bringing to this book a perspective influenced by my beliefs. If you are not of that particular faith, keep in mind that this principle of being prepared temporally is something that applies to everyone. My faith strives for self-reliance, and focuses on all aspects of preparedness, not just temporal.

Having a functioning food storage is only one of the ways in which we can make sure we're being prepared. I have not focused on the other areas that The Church of Jesus Christ of Latter-day Saints recommends being prepared in. For more information on the other areas you can be better prepared in, look to the church materials, the church leader's council, and the church's website devoted to this topic. (www.providentliving.org)

A Few Other Areas To Prepared In

- Spiritual Preparations (know and love those scriptures)
- Non-Food Storage Items (clothing, toiletries, etc.)
- Having A Financial Reserve and Being Debt Free (can't stress that enough)
- Medicine and Vitamins (adequate amounts of each)
- Education (it's so important to gain an education and to learn as much as we can)
- Gardening and Preserving (learn how to and do it regularly)
- Self-Reliance (learn how to be independent)
- 72 Hour Kits (update them regularly)
- . . . just to name a few!

Chapter 3

Recommended Tools

Recommended Tools For Recipes

- Can Opener
- Cast Iron Skillets (a 12" for sure, with lid)
- Cooking Utensils (no stainless steel on cast iron)
- Dutch Ovens (with lids)
- Food Containers
- Large Soup Pot (with lid)
- Mason Jars (with lids)
- Measuring Cups & Spoons
- Mess Kits (with silverware)
- Mortar & Pestle
- Mixing Bowls (with lids)
- Spatulas, Ladles & Strong Whisks
- Sharp Knives
- Stainless Steel Box Grater
- Stainless Steel & Non-Stick Pots & Pans (with lids)
- Strainers (fine mesh & colanders)
- Vegetable Peeler

Recommended Tools For Cleaning Recipes

- Bucket (for laundry)
- Mason Jars (with lids)
- Measuring Cups & Spoons
- Squirt Bottles
- Toothbrushes
- Washcloths

Recommended Tools For Herbal Remedies

- Candy Molds
- Cotton Balls
- Cookie Sheet (or flat tray)
- Cooking Utensils
- Fabric Strips (for making wraps, applying compresses or poultices)
- Mason Jars (with lids)
- Mesh Strainers
- Measuring Cups & Spoons
- Mortar & Pestle
- Muslin Fabric (works as a strainer & covering when steeping ingredients)
- Pots (with lids)
- Sharp Knives
- Spatulas, Ladles & Strong Whisks
- Stainless Steel Box Grater
- Vegetable Peeler
- Tea Pot & Tea Balls
- Wax Paper

Cooking Tips

How to Cook Grains

WHEAT

In a medium saucepan, bring 1 qt. of water to a boil. Once boiling, add 1 c. wheat berries. Reduce the heat to a simmer, cover the pan, and let cook for about 40 minutes, until the berries are soft and chewy but not mushy. Then strain and keep in an air tight container. They will not last long unrefrigerated, so it's best to make only enough for your meals that you are preparing that day.

BARLEY

In a medium saucepan, bring 1 qt. of water to a boil. Once boiling, add 1 c. barley. Reduce the heat to a simmer, cover the pan, and let cook for about 30 minutes, until the barley is soft and chewy but not mushy. Then strain and keep in an air tight container. It will not last long unrefrigerated, so it's best to make only enough for your meals that you are preparing that day.

SPELT

In a medium saucepan, bring 1 qt. of water to a boil. Once boiling, add 1 c. spelt. Reduce the heat to a simmer, cover the pan, and let cook for about 45 minutes, until the spelt is soft and chewy but not mushy. Then strain and keep in an air tight container. It will not last long unrefrigerated, so it's best to make only enough for your meals that you are preparing that day.

RICE

In a medium saucepan, bring 1 qt. of water to a boil. Once boiling, add 1 c. rice. Let the rice gently boil for about 7-10 minutes (about 15 minutes for brown rice). Taste test the rice to see how long it needs to cook . . . basmati rice cooks faster than the LDS Cannery white rice. Strain, then fluff, then keep in an air tight container. It will not last long unrefrigerated, so it's best to make only enough for your meals that you are preparing that day.

Sweeteners

In this book, I have listed sugar in many recipes. This is cost-effective for many people to store, as well as providing some additional calories while camping. However, please use whatever you feel comfortable with. There are many alternatives to sugar, and this is where customizing for your family's needs comes in.

Flour

When flour is called for in my recipes, I am referring to all-purpose flour. This is also very practical and cost-effective to store. If you have a hand grinder and wheat, then you can easily exchange whole wheat flour for many of these recipes. Experiment and see if you want to use half and half or incorporate your own gluten-free mixes and alternative flours. It will take tweaking, but these recipes are a great spring board to see what you prefer for your family.

Oil

I don't specify which oil to use in my recipes. Let this be your choice of what you're comfortable with. Whether it's vegetable, olive, coconut, or another one, they will all work fine in these recipes.

How To Cook Over A Wood Burning Stove

This is a bit tricky because it is subject to change. Your cooking depends on how hot your fire is in your stove. It's hard to adjust for temperature like you would with a conventional stovetop burner. I've found that layering canning rings under your skillet or pot is very useful. Each layer provides more space from the direct heat. As you can imagine, placing your skillet directly upon the wood stove would be high heat, adding a layer of canning rings would be medium to medium high (depending on the heat of your stove), adding another layer would be low to medium low, and so forth. This will take some experimenting to see how many rings to add to keep your soups simmering and not boiling. Like I mentioned in the introduction, this book is meant to be utilized right now as you're camping and experimenting. As you learn to cook over a wood burning stove, add your notes in the margins of this book and make it your own.

How To Cook Over An Open Fire

When cooking over an open fire, remember that it's the coals (not the flames) that will cook your food evenly. Keeping a skillet or pot directly over the coals will be the highest heat. As you elevate your skillet, the amount of heat will decrease. This isn't something you can put into the amount of inches to correspond with direct temperatures. It depends on how hot your coals are. This will take practice to see how high off the coals you need to raise your food for the right temperature. Getting tools to prop your pots over a fire, or grills that are made for campfire cooking, is ideal in this situation.

A Note About Traditional Cooking Methods Mentioned In This Book

As previously noted, this book is to start cooking with now to see what your family likes and to make it yours. I realize that you can't go camping every week throughout the year. I have provided how to cook many of these dishes using standard heat measurements (high, medium, low) so you can make these recipes now in your home. These are meals you can enjoy year round, whether outside camping or inside cooking.

Cooking With Cast Iron Cookware

The real trick to cooking with cast iron is the heat! If you're cooking breakfast pancakes, breads or baking, use low heat. Cast iron cookware retains its heat very well, so you don't need to get it too hot to cook evenly. Low heat is better, or else you will burn your food! When cooking tortillas or soups, you can go a little warmer and stay on medium heat. You will find the right temperature as you experiment with this cookware. Cast iron is a great option because of its ease to clean, even cooking, and very durable capabilities. The cast iron items you buy, if seasoned right and carefully maintained, will last for generations.

Conversion Chart For Basic Measurements In This Book

3 tsp = 1 Tbsp
4 Tbsp = 1/4 cup
2 cups = 1 pint
4 cups = 1 quart
4 quarts = 1 gallon

Chapter 4

Breakfasts

- Oatmeal
- Cream of Wheat
- Couscous Cereal
- Granola
- Biscuits and Gravy
- Coconut Pancakes
- Flap Jacks
- Fluffy Pancakes

- Crepes
- Wheat Berries
- Barley Bowls
- Spelt Porridge
- Maple Syrup
- Coconut Syrup
- Coconut Cream

The whole grain berries in this section have been prepared in three different ways. You can cook most whole grains using these ideas, but feel free to switch it up and try your own variations!

If you are gluten intolerant, use other grains and seeds that are gluten free and certified (like Amaranth, Teff, Oat Groats, Job's Tears, Millet, Quinoa, and Rice, for example).

Many of the items in this book are available at LDS Canneries. However, for grocery items and grains that aren't sold there, you can usually special order them through your local grocery store or health food store in bulk quantities, as well as other bulk food storage suppliers.

Enhance any breakfast with other foods you store, such as: Canned Meats, Canned Milks, Dried Fruits, Sauces, Spices, Syrups, Canned Preserves, etc.

Make some these recipes sweet or savory depending on what your family prefers!

Oatmeal

1 qt. Water (4 c.)
2 c. Rolled Oats
1/4 c. Sugar
1/4 c. Brown Sugar
1 Tbs. Vanilla

Bring water to a boil, add the rolled oats and cook for about 5-6 minutes. You want the oats to be soft and cooked through, but not mushy. If you hand rolled your oats (using an oat roller), then you will need to cook them for a couple minutes longer. Once the oats are thick, add the sugars and vanilla. Serve warm. Makes about 4 c.

 Add any spices to change up the flavor, like cinnamon, nutmeg, etc. Mix in any dried fruits, too. You can also thin this out with a little milk to feed more. Use prepared milk or evaporated milk.

Cream of Wheat

1 qt. Water (4 c.)
2/3 c. Cream of Wheat
1/4 c. Sugar
1/4 c. Brown Sugar
1 Tbs. Vanilla

Bring the water to a boil. Add the cream of wheat slowly, stirring the entire time. You don't want any lumps. Reduce the heat, stirring continually. Once the wheat thickens, add the sugars and vanilla.

 Once it's done, you can thin it out to feed more with milk. Either use prepared milk or evaporated milk, but keep in mind that a little goes a long way. Add any spices as well to change up the flavor (cinnamon, nutmeg, etc.).

Coconut Couscous

1 (13.6 oz.) can Coconut Milk
1/4 c. Sugar
1 tsp. Vanilla
1 c. Couscous

In a medium pan, bring the coconut milk and sugar to a boil. Once the milk starts to foam, add the vanilla and couscous. Cover the pan and remove from the heat. Let sit for 10 minutes, then uncover and fluff. This makes a great and creamy breakfast. Add in any mix-in's you prefer.

Granola

1/2 c. Maple Syrup	1/2 tsp. Salt
1/2 c. Brown Sugar	1 Tbs. Pumpkin Pie Spice
1/2 c. Vegetable Oil	5 c. Rolled Oats
1 Tbs. Vanilla	

Mix everything well together in a large bowl. Over medium heat, stir the granola in a cast iron skillet. Stir occasionally (so the oats don't burn) until everything is toasted. Let cool, then store in air tight containers (like mason jars).

 This is a crunchy and dry granola. Use as a cold cereal with milk or by itself. Mix in any dried fruit you prefer.

Biscuits and Gravy

Buttermilk Drop Biscuits
Milk Gravy

Pour the gravy over top of these biscuits.

I almost didn't put this recipe in. It's so simple to combine the two, but my southern roots and my husband both convinced me to keep it.

This is one of my husband's favorite breakfast meals. He loves this version and I have to agree, it tastes pretty amazing. This is a classic southern breakfast and makes a great supper as well!

If you have any meat you want to crumble into the gravy, it gives it even more flavor.

Coconut Pancakes

2 c. Flour
1/2 c. Sugar
1/2 tsp. Salt
4 tsp. Baking Powder

1/2 c. Water
1 (13.6 oz.) can
   Coconut Milk
1 Tbs. Vanilla

In a medium bowl, combine all the dry ingredients. Make a well in the middle and pour in the wet ingredients. Mix until combined, but don't over mix .

Warm up a skillet or griddle over medium heat. Brush it with a light coat of oil. Scoop the batter onto the hot skillet about 1/4 c. at a time. Once bubbles form, flip then cook the other side until golden brown. Makes about 16 pancakes. These are great with some coconut syrup on top!

Flap Jacks

1 1/2 c. Whole
   Wheat Flour
1 Tbs. Baking Powder
1/2 tsp. Salt

2 Tbs. Sugar
2 Tbs. Oil
1 1/2 c. Milk

In a medium bowl, combine all the dry ingredients. Make a well in the middle and pour in the wet ingredients. Mix until combined, but don't over mix .

Warm up a skillet or griddle over medium heat. Brush it with a light coat of oil. Scoop the batter onto the hot skillet about 1/4 c. at a time. Once bubbles form, flip then cook the other side until golden brown. Makes about 6 flap jacks.

Fluffy Pancakes

1 1/2 c. Flour   1/2 tsp. Salt
1 Tbs. Baking Powder   1 c. Milk
2 Tbs. Sugar   1/4 c. Oil

In a medium bowl, combine all the dry ingredients. Make a well in the middle and pour in the wet ingredients. Mix until combined, but don't over mix .

Warm up a skillet or griddle over medium heat. Brush it with a light coat of oil. Scoop the batter onto the hot skillet about 1/4 c. at a time. Once bubbles form, flip then cook the other side until golden brown. Makes about 6 pancakes.

Crepes

1 c. Flour	1/2 c. Milk
1 Tbs. Sugar	2/3 c. Water
1/4 tsp. Salt	1/4 c. Oil

In a medium bowl, combine all the dry ingredients. Make a well in the middle and pour in the wet ingredients. Mix until combined, but don't over mix .

Warm up a non-stick 8" pan. Heat up the pan over medium-low heat. Brush with a light coat of oil. Scoop the batter onto the hot pan about 1/3 c. at a time. Swirl the batter around the pan until it's completely coated. Once bubbles form (wait a minute or two until it's lightly golden on the bottom), flip then cook the other side. Makes about 6 crepes.

 These are most often eaten with Nutella spread on them, then wrapped up like a parcel. Fill with whatever you'd like (canned fruit, Coconut Cream, meats, etc.)!

As the French say, "La premiere crepe est pour le chien." Which means, "The first pancake is for the dog." In the US we say, "If at first you don't succeed, keep trying." The first crepe is always the hardest!

Wheat Berries with Cinnamon Sugar

1 qt. Water (4 c.)
1 c. Wheat Berries (red or white)
Cinnamon Sugar
Milk

In a medium saucepan, bring the water and wheat to a boil. Reduce the heat and simmer with the lid on for 40 minutes. Strain and top the cooked wheat berries with Cinnamon Sugar and milk, or some Coconut Cream!

Barley Bowls with Coconut Cream

1 qt. Water (4 c.)
1 c. Barley
Coconut Cream

In a medium saucepan, bring the water and barley to a boil. Reduce the heat and simmer with the lid on for 30 minutes. Strain and top the barley with some Cinnamon Sugar and milk, or some Coconut Cream!

Spelt Porridge

1 (13.6 oz.) can Coconut Milk
2 Cinnamon Sticks
1 c. Water
1 c. Spelt
1/4 c. Sugar

In a medium saucepan, bring the coconut milk, water and cinnamon sticks to a boil, stirring constantly. Once boiling, add the spelt. Reduce the heat and cover. Let simmer for 45-60 minutes, until the spelt is very soft and tender, stirring occasionally. If some of the spelt bursts, that is okay. Spoon out the cinnamon sticks, add the sugar, and stir until dissolved.

Maple Syrup

1 c. Water
1 c. Sugar
1 c. Brown Sugar
1 Tbs. Maple Extract
1 Tbs. Vanilla

In a large pan (because the sugars could boil over if your heat is too high), add the water and the sugars. Boil until the sugars are all dissolved. Cook for about 3 minutes on a gentle boil. Remove from heat and add the extracts, stirring well. This will slightly thicken as it cools. Makes about 1 pint.

 To make this stretch further, you can thin it out by doubling the amount of water. It will be a thinner syrup, but can make everything last a bit longer.

Coconut Syrup

1 (13.6 oz.) can Coconut Milk
1/4 c. Sugar
1 tsp. Vanilla

In a medium pan, bring everything to a boil, stirring constantly. Let boil for a few minutes, then remove from the heat. Once cooled, store in a mason jar. Make in small batches since this won't keep without refrigeration. Makes about 1 pint.

Coconut Cream

2 Tbs. Cornstarch
1 (13.6 oz.) can Coconut Milk
1/4 c. Sugar
1 tsp. Vanilla

In a medium pan, bring everything to a boil. Let cook for a few minutes until everything starts to thicken. Remove from heat and stir. This will thicken as it cools. Makes about 1 pint.

 This is a delicious light cream sauce that is perfect over fresh cooked grains, or a filling for crepes!

Chapter 5

Lunch Ideas

For lunch, you can go simple. This might change depending on where you live, the climate you're in, and what you're doing during the day.

You can also make the midday meal the largest meal of the day (your typical supper recipe), and go light for dinner (eating leftovers and bread).

There's no rule that says you can't make a breakfast recipe for lunch as well. You can also let this meal be the quick and easy one of the day by making a quick bread with a simple side dish.

Take any of these ideas and incorporate them at your comfort level. There is no one way to incorporate food storage into daily living.

- Cornbread and Fruit
- Tortillas and Beans
- Farls and Gravy
- Biscuits and Fruit
- Leftovers
- Make Any Breakfast or Supper Recipe

Snack Ideas

Snacks are not meant to be another meal . . . more something to tide the hunger over from the day until mealtime. This can be something small but satisfying and doesn't require a lot of prep or time to eat. For children especially, it is important to have something on their stomachs. Their metabolism is usually very rapid and requires a lot more energy as they are growing.

Snacks can be simple. Using any side dish, leftovers, or something as simple as biscuits or bread can double as a snack.

Snacks are best between the hours of lunch and supper, anytime around the mid-part of the afternoon. Usually one snack per day can be enough, but that amount can vary.

- Crackers (Graham, Animal, Whole Grain)
- Anything from the Side Dish Ideas
- Apple Slices and Dried Fruit
- Biscuits, Breads, and Dried Pretzels
- Candy (hard ones like Dum-Dum Suckers, Butterscotch, Peppermints, etc.)

Side Dish Ideas

If you are able to home can your own food, that's great! If not, it's better to purchase them from the store than to have nothing at all. I'm not sure how practical side dishes will be if you are long-term camping. They may become a meal in and of themselves. However, if your storage space permits, I have included some ideas to get you thinking about what your family might enjoy to help supplement your meals and snack ideas.

Look for sales at your local grocery stores, bulk order with friends, or better yet, grow and can these items yourself. If you don't have a garden or a means for one, see if someone would be willing to share the work and the harvest with your family. Many community gardens have benefited lots of families who otherwise wouldn't be able to have one. You can home can meats, fruits, and vegetables. You can also pickle eggs, garlic, vegetables, and meats. Those items will be a delight when camping, as well as pack a nutritional powerhouse of vitamins and minerals.

Fermented and pickled foods add a great benefit to our health and are great items to remember.

These are just some ideas that I have used as side dishes. Feel free to use any vegetables in the canned foods section of your grocery store that you like! You can use the Spice Blends in this book to season and enjoy your vegetables with. You can also eat the fruit right out of the can, and drink any juices that are leftover. Just start looking on those grocery shelves when you're stocking your pantry! There are a lot more things you can add to this list. The main suggestion is to try these foods out now and see what you want to stock up on. For more information about how to preserve and pickle foods, contact your local county cooperative extension office.

- Asparagus
- Black Olives
- Beans
- Beets (regular or pickled)
- Fruit (all varieties, canned or dried)
- Green Olives
- Green Beans
- Peas
- Pickles
- Pickled Eggs, Garlic, Meats, and Vegetables
- Potatoes
- Sauerkraut
- Yams

Drinks

- Fruit Drink Mix
- Hot Cocoa Mix
- Powdered Milk
- Chocolate Milk
- Herbal Chai
- Golden Milk

Having a variety of drinks is a wonderful addition to your food storage. Not only does it taste delicious, but if the water that you have on hand isn't as tasty as you would desire, these mixes can really help enhance its flavor. You can find these drink mixes and obtain powdered milk at your local LDS cannery.

The instructions for these drink mixes are specified on the #10 can label from the LDS Cannery. Feel free to adjust the measurements according to your preference. Store as much as your family requires, as that amount will depend on each individual family's needs.

Fruit Drink Mix

1 c. Fruit Drink Mix
2 qt. (8 c.) Water

 Add 1 tsp. Vanilla to make it taste even better.

Hot Cocoa Mix

3/4 c. Cocoa Mix
1 qt. (4 c.) Hot Water

Individual Serving:
3 Tbs. Cocoa Mix
1 c. Hot Water

Powdered Milk

For amounts needed to reconstitute, please reference the Dry Milk Conversion Chart on page 37.

 Add 1 tsp. Sugar or Honey per gallon.

We've enjoyed flavoring our powdered milk for special treats!

Chocolate Milk

1/2 c. Hot Cocoa Mix
2 qt. Milk

Whisk together well. If you can, store it in a cool place overnight. If not, drink right away.

Herbal Chai

2 c. Milk
1-2 Cinnamon Sticks
1 heaping tsp. Peppercorns
1/4 heaping tsp. Whole Cloves
5 Green Cardamom Pods
1-2 Tbs. Sugar or Honey

Cook the milk and spices together in a saucepan on low heat for about 15 minutes or until the milk foams, stirring constantly. Strain the spices out, then add your sweetener.

Golden Milk

2 c. Milk
1/2 tsp. Turmeric
1-2 Tbs. Sugar or Honey

Put all the ingredients in a quart sized mason jar and screw a lid on tightly. Shake well until everything is incorporated. It may be a little gritty, but this is wonderful for inflammation, arthritis, swelling in the joints, or other aches and pains.

A great way to use powdered milk is to add the dry milk to your dry ingredients, and then the proper amount of water to reconstitute it with the wet ingredients. That way you can make just the amount you need without wasting anything.

Breakdown of LDS Cannery Nonfat Dry Milk

Have you ever wanted to make just enough milk to cook with in a recipe? Now you can! These conversions are based off the LDS Cannery's #10 can of nonfat dry milk. The ratios will be different for other brands. I usually round up a little when using this chart because having a little extra powder in your recipes will be fine. This always tastes the best icy cold, but if you have to drink it warm, try adding some flavoring to give it a better taste.

Amount of Milk	Water	Powder
1 Tbsp	1 Tbsp	1/2 tsp + 1/8 tsp
2 Tbsp	2 Tbsp	1 tsp + 1/4 tsp
3 Tbsp	3 Tbsp	2 tsp
1/4 cup	1/4 cup	2 tsp + 1/2 tsp
1/3 cup	1/3 cup	1 Tbsp
1/2 cup	1/2 cup	5 tsp
2/3 cup	2/3 cup	2 Tbsp
3/4 cup	3/4 cup	2 Tbsp + 3/4 tsp
1 cup	1 cup	3 Tbsp
2 cups	2 cups	1/4 cup + 2 Tbsp
3 cups	3 cups	1/2 cup + 1 Tbsp
1 quart	4 cups	3/4 cup
2 quarts	8 cups	1 cup + 1/2 cup
1 gallon	4 quarts	3 cups

Chapter 6

Breads

- Cornbread
- Buttermilk Biscuits
- Irish Soda Bread (Farl)
- Bannock
- Flour Tortillas
- Corn Tortillas

Ghee is a delicious clarified butter product, usually already bottled in glass jars. You can sometimes find it in the international section or health food section at the store, and it's available at Indian grocery stores or online. You can put Ghee on your breads and top with honey!

Cornbread

5 Tbs. Powdered Milk	1 tsp. Baking Powder
1 c. Cornmeal	1 tsp. Baking Soda
1 c. Flour	1 1/2 c. Water
1/2 c. Sugar	1 Tbs. Vinegar
1/2 tsp. Salt	(apple cider or white)

Mix all the dry ingredients in a large bowl together. Then add in the water and vinegar. Mix well. Let sit for about 5 minutes.

Heat a cast iron skillet over low heat. Then pour the thin batter into a large cast iron skillet. Put the lid on and let cook for about 20-25 minutes. Uncover and make sure the bread is cooked in the middle before serving. It may need a few more minutes with the lid off.

Biscuits

2 c. Flour	1 tsp. Salt
1 Tbs. Baking Powder	1/3 c. Oil
2 Tbs. Sugar	2/3 c. Milk

Mix all the dry ingredients well in a large bowl. Make a well in the middle, then pour in the oil and milk. Mix until the batter comes together (don't over mix).

Heat a cast iron skillet over low heat. Drop large spoonfuls onto a greased skillet, then place the lid on. Let cook for about 10 minutes, then carefully flip and cook for another 10 minutes.

These work best by not crowding the skillet. Only cook a few at a time so you can flip them easily. The key is to keep your temperature low!

Irish Soda Bread (Farl)

1 1/2 c. Milk (a few Tbsp more if needed)
1 Tbs. Vinegar
2 1/2 c. Flour + 1/2 c. Flour (divided)

1 tsp. Baking Soda
1/2 tsp. Salt

Mix the milk and the vinegar, then let sit for a few minutes. In a medium bowl, mix all the dry ingredients together well so there are no clumps. Add in the wet ingredients, then mix well (it will be slightly sticky). Add extra 1/2 c. flour if needed. The dough shouldn't be too sticky.

On a flat surface, knead the dough a few times. Then shape into a circle or square. Cut the pieces of dough into 4 pie-shaped pieces. Place these on a skillet over low heat (any hotter and you'll burn the bread).

Let the bread toast, moving it around occasionally so it doesn't stick and burn. After about 10 minutes, flip then cook the other side for about 10 more minutes.

 This is a skillet-style bread used a very long time ago as the original way to cook Irish soda bread in Ireland. Cut down the middles and add a topping or eat plain.

Bannock

3 1/2 c. Flour   1/4 c. Oil
1 tsp. Salt   1 1/2 c. Water
2 Tbs. Baking Powder

Heat a 12-inch cast iron skillet over low heat. In a large bowl, mix together the dry ingredients. Add in the oil and water. Combine with your hands until a dough ball forms. Knead for a few minutes until it's well incorporated. Flatten out into a round disc. Place it on a warmed cast iron skillet. Let it cook for about 15 minutes on each side.

 The trick to making great bannock is having your skillet the right temperature. It has to be on low heat or you will burn the bread.

This is a very old Scottish bread. It was originally made with barley or oatmeal dough. It was first recorded in the 15th century and we're still making it today!

Flour Tortillas

2 c. Flour
1/2 tsp. Salt
1/4 tsp. Baking Powder
1/4 c. Oil
1/2 c. Hot Water

In a medium bowl, mix the dry ingredients together. Then add in the wet ingredients. Mix together well with your hands. Knead until a dough ball forms. You may need to add a few more tablespoons of water if it is a little dry.

Cut into 8 even pieces. Roll each piece into a ball. Keep covered with a damp cloth. Press with a tortilla press or roll out into 1/4 inch tortillas.

In a cast iron skillet over medium heat, cook the tortilla for a few minutes on each side. Flip when you see golden brown spots. Keep in a warmer or eat right away.

 These are not as flexible as store bought tortillas unless you roll them very thin. We enjoy them thicker and eat them more like flat breads all the time.

Corn Tortillas

1 c. Flour
1 c. Masa Corn Flour
1/2 tsp. Salt
1/4 tsp. Baking Powder
1/4 c. Oil
3/4 c. Hot Water

In a medium bowl, mix the dry ingredients together. Then add in the wet ingredients. Mix together well with your hands. Knead until a dough ball forms. You may need to add a few more tablespoons of water if it is a little dry.

Cut into 8 even pieces. Roll each piece into a ball. Keep covered with a damp cloth. Press with a tortilla press or roll out into 1/4 inch tortillas.

In a cast iron skillet over medium heat, cook the tortilla for a few minutes on each side. Flip when you see golden brown spots. Keep in a warmer or eat right away.

Masa Corn Flour is a finely ground corn flour that can be found in the international, baking, or Hispanic sections of most grocery stores. These are not as flexible as store bought tortillas unless you roll them very thin. We enjoy them thicker and eat them more like flat breads all the time.

Chapter 7

Spice Blends & Gravy

- Pumpkin Pie Spice
- Cinnamon Sugar
- Poultry Seasoning
- Seasoning Salt
- Taco Seasoning

- Mild Curry Blend
- Herbs de Provence
- Hearty Soup Blend
- Chicken Gravy
- Milk Gravy

Why store lots of pre-made spice blends when you can make your own? Making your own blends is easy and you can tweak them just the way your family prefers. Add a pinch of these blends to any number of meals and see just how much better they taste with a boost of flavor from simple spices and herbs!

Use "Parts"

When making up a blend, you can use whatever parts you want. Keep the ratio's the same and it will turn out great. For example, if it says 1 part, then that is the original measurement you've chosen (say a Tbsp. for example). Then if the recipe says use a half-part, simply use half of your original measurement (that would be half a Tbsp.). You can use a Tbsp., tsp., or any measuring cup for a part. This means you can make any blend you want for any size container you have. I always store my blends in glass jars. They last a long time stored this way and always taste great!

Pumpkin Pie Spice

1 tsp. Cinnamon
1/2 tsp. Ginger
1/4 tsp. Nutmeg
1/8 tsp. Cloves

Add all the spices into a mason jar and shake well. This can stay stored in a mason jar for months!

 I'm a big pumpkin pie fan. Having tasted many a spice blend in my day, I have to say this is head and shoulders above anything that's out there! It's great mixed with sugar sprinkled on toast or fried dough!

Cinnamon Sugar

2 Tbs. Cinnamon
2 tsp. Sugar
1/4 tsp. Nutmeg

Add all the spices into a mason jar and shake well. This can stay stored in a mason jar for months!

 This is the perfect topping to desserts, breads, or cooked whole grains if you want a sweet treat.

Poultry Seasoning

1 Tbs. Rosemary   1 Tbs. Thyme
1 Tbs. Oregano   1 tsp. Sage
1 Tbs. Ginger   1 tsp. Pepper
1 Tbs. Marjoram

Mix well, then grind very fine with a mortar and pestle. This can stay stored in a mason jar for months!

This is based off the Bell's Poultry Seasoning blend. It's some of the best-tasting poultry seasoning you can get, and it's only sold in the New England area. This is fantastic cooked with any poultry!

Seasoning Salt

1 Tbs. Salt
1 tsp. Sugar
1/2 tsp. Paprika
1/4 tsp. Turmeric

1/4 tsp. Onion Powder
1/4 tsp. Garlic Powder
1/4 tsp. Celery Salt
1/4 tsp. Cornstarch

Add all the spices into a mason jar and shake well. This can stay stored in a mason jar for months!

 This knocks the socks off Lawry's Seasoning Salt, plus you can adjust the seasonings to your own preference. Add this to anything and everything!

Taco Seasoning

2 tsp. Garlic Powder
2 tsp. Onion Powder
2 tsp. Oregano
1 tsp. Cumin

1 tsp. Pepper
1/2 tsp. Salt
1/2 tsp. Coriander

Add all the spices into a mason jar and shake well. This can stay stored in a mason jar for months!

Mild Curry Blend

1 Tbs. Turmeric	1/2 tsp. Salt
2 tsp. Coriander	1/4 tsp. Ground Fennel
1 tsp. Cumin	Seed

Add all the spices into a mason jar and shake well. This can stay stored in a mason jar for months!

We have loved India's culture and food so much! There is nothing like having these spices simmering away to take you across oceans and into amazing dishes and flavors! Indian cooking uses many spices and has wonderful complexity in its layers of flavors. Having your own house blend makes cooking a lot faster and more toward your taste preference.

Herbs de Provence

5 Tbs. Savory (the whole dried herb, not ground)	1 Tbs. Rosemary
	1 Tbs. Thyme
3 Tbs. Oregano	1 Tbs. Lavender

Make sure these are all whole dried spices and not the ground versions. Add all the spices into a mason jar and shake well. This can stay stored in a mason jar for months!

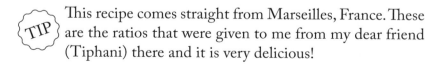 This recipe comes straight from Marseilles, France. These are the ratios that were given to me from my dear friend (Tiphani) there and it is very delicious!

Herbs de Provence has an interesting history. It's not actually French at all, but a commercial blend that was created in the USA during the 1970s. It helped boost sales to make the blend sound more French and using herbs typical of Provincial cooking.

During my time in France, I learned a lot about herbs. The French don't use herbs just because they taste good . . . they use herbs because they are healthy for you!

Hearty Soup Blend

1 Tbs. Dehydrated Onion	1 tsp. Rosemary
1 tsp. Salt	1/2 tsp. Pepper
1 tsp. Oregano	1/2 tsp. Garlic Powder

Using a mortar and pestle, grind the rosemary and oregano together until finely ground. Then add all the spices and onion into a mason jar and shake well. This can stay stored in a mason jar for months!

Chicken Gravy

2 c. Water	1/4 c. Water
1 Chicken Bouillon Cube	2 Tbs. Flour
1 tsp. Poultry Seasoning	1 pint Canned Chicken
1/4 tsp. Salt	(with juices)

In a medium saucepan, combine the 2 c. water, bouillon, seasoning and salt. Bring to a boil.

Meanwhile, in a bowl, break up your chicken with a fork so it's shredded evenly. Mix your flour and water together in a mason jar and shake until they are well combined. Once the gravy is boiling, slowly whisk in the flour mixture. Once it thickens, stir in the chicken and reduce the heat. Stir until the chicken is warmed through.

Milk Gravy

1/4 c. Oil
1 (12 oz.) can Evaporated
  Milk
1 1/2 c. Water

1/3 c. Flour
2 tsp. Seasoning Salt
1 tsp. Pepper

In a medium saucepan over medium heat, whisk the milk and the oil together constantly. You can use the empty can from the evaporated milk, for your measurement of water, or just add 1 1/2 c. water. Combine the water with the flour, and whisk together well.

Once the milk starts to froth, whisk in the flour mixture slowly. Bring to a boil, and cook for about 1 or 2 more minutes, until it thickens. Remove from the heat. Add the Seasoning Salt and pepper, adjusting to your taste preference.

You can add any meat to this that you'd like, or enjoy it without any meat, which is how we typically eat it. Most canned meats can be crumbled into this really well. This is a great all-purpose gravy to pour over potatoes, meats, veggies, biscuits, toast, and more!

Chapter 8

Suppers

Supper is a term I chose specifically. As we're used to calling the evening meal "dinner," it congers up thoughts of meat and potatoes, with a roll, a few side dishes and a tall glass of milk, usually followed by a yummy dessert. Camping doesn't enable you to feast like the typical dinners we're used to. Suppers usually refer to a lighter and much simpler meal.

Suppers are a great simple meal to have. You might find it better to have supper as a mid-day meal and go light on your evening meal. You may prefer to have supper when the day is done and go lighter for the mid-day meal. Either way is fine, just do whatever suits your schedule and family needs best.

Having side dishes with every meal, enough to have friends over to share with, and a dessert following most evenings isn't always practical while camping on food storage. I wanted to include a lot of soups and dishes that could feed a lot of people or a smaller family. As you try these recipes out, see what your family likes. Could you enjoy these while camping? Customize these recipes and tweak them any way you want!

- Bacon Bits
- Canned Foods
- Canned Meats
- Condiments
- Sauces
- Spices, etc.

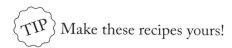 Make these recipes yours!

Soups, Chowder & Stews

- Creamy Tomato Soup
- Hearty 5 Bean Soup
- Indian Dahl
- Turkish Lentil Soup
- Split Pea Soup

- Taco Soup
- Creamy Chicken Soup
- Corn Chowder
- Lentil Stew
- Wheat Berry Chili

There is nothing quite as comforting as a warm pot of soup! These recipes are easy to double. You can also add more water if you want to stretch your soup out more. Get creative and add whatever you want! These recipes are easy to add to and build from to create even more nourishing combinations for your taste buds.

Creamy Tomato Soup

1 qt. Water (4 c.)
1 (8 oz.) can Tomato Sauce
1 (14.5 oz.) can Diced
  Tomatoes
2 tsp. Salt

2 tsp. Hearty Soup Blend
1 Tbs. Sugar
1 (12 oz.) can Evaporated
  Milk

Add all the ingredients except the evaporated milk into a medium pot. Cook over medium heat until it's all cooked through. Then stir in the evaporated milk and serve immediately.

Hearty Five Bean Soup

1/2 c. Dry Pinto Beans
1/2 c. Dry Split Green Peas
1/2 c. Dry Great Northern
  Beans
1/2 c. Dry Black Beans
1/2 c. Dry Kidney Beans
1 Chicken Bouillon Cube

1 Tbs. Hearty Soup Blend
1-2 Bay Leaves
2 qt. Water (8 c.)
1 (14.5 oz.) can Diced
  Tomatoes
Salt

Put all the dry beans in a large pot. Cover with water about 2 inches over the beans. Bring to a boil. Remove from the heat, then put the lid on and let sit for 1 hour. Strain out the water.

Add:
Chicken Bouillon Cube, Hearty Soup Blend, Bay Leaves
2 qt. Water (8 c.)

Bring to a boil, then simmer for 1 to 1 & 1/2 hours, or until the beans are tender but not mushy. Add the diced tomatoes and salt to your taste preference.

Indian Dahl

1 qt. Water (4 c.)
2 Chicken Bouillon Cubes
2 c. Dry Red Lentils
1 Tbs. Sugar
1 tsp. Turmeric
1 tsp. Coriander
1 tsp. Mild Curry Blend

1 tsp. Cumin
1/2 tsp. Salt
1 (14.5 oz.) can Diced
   Tomatoes
1 (13.6 oz.) can Coconut
   Milk

In a medium pot over medium heat, cook all the ingredients except the tomatoes and coconut milk. Stir occasionally, and cook for about 15 minutes, or until the lentils are soft, but not mushy (this should look thick and creamy). Then add in the tomatoes and the coconut milk and serve warm.

 We like eating this with flat bread and use it to mop up anything left in the bowls. The Flour Tortillas work great for this.

Split Pea Soup

2 qt. Water (8 c.)
2 c. Split Green Peas
2 Chicken Bouillon Cubes
1 (14.5 oz.) can Corn
1 (5 oz.) can Water
   Chestnuts

1 (14.5 oz.) can Whole
   Potatoes, drained and
   quartered
1 Tbs. Hearty Soup Blend

Bring the water to a boil and reduce the heat. Add the split peas and the chicken bouillon and let simmer for 40 minutes, or until the peas are tender. Then add in the corn, water chestnuts, potatoes, and spices, warm through, and serve.

Turkish Lentil Soup

2 qt. Water (8 c.)   1 Tbs. Cumin
2 Chicken Bouillon Cubes   1 tsp. Salt
2 c. Dry Green Lentils   1/4 tsp. Pepper
2 Tbs. Dehydrated Onions   Lemon Juice
1/2 tsp. Garlic Powder
1 (14.5 oz.) can Diced
   Tomatoes

In a large pot, add the water, chicken bouillon, lentils, onion, garlic powder, and tomatoes. Bring to a boil, then reduce the heat to a simmer for about 45 minutes, or until the lentils are tender, stirring occasionally.

Once the lentils are soft, add the spices, and stir until it's all combined. Serve hot, and add a squeeze of lemon juice over the top of the lentils in your bowl.

Taco Soup

1 qt. Water (4 c.)   1 (14.5 oz.) can Kidney
2 Beef Bouillon Cubes   Beans, drained and rinsed
1 c. Cooked Wheat Berries   1 (14.5 oz.) can Black
1 (2.25 oz.) can Sliced   Beans, drained & rinsed
   Olives, drained   1 Tbs. Taco Seasoning
1 (14.5 oz.) can Diced
   Tomatoes

In a large pot, combine all the ingredients. Warm through and serve.

Creamy Chicken Soup

3 c. Water + 1 c. Water
(divided)
2 Chicken Bouillon cubes
1/4 tsp. Poultry Seasoning
1/4 tsp. Onion Powder
1/4 tsp. Garlic Powder
1/4 tsp. Pepper
1/4 tsp. Salt
1/4 tsp. Parsley
6 Tbs. Flour
1 pint canned Chicken
(with juices)
1 (12 oz.) can Evaporated
Milk

Over medium heat, bring 3 c. water, bouillon cubes, Poultry Seasoning and spices, and bring to a gentle boil. Meanwhile, mix the remaining 1 c. water and the flour together until there are no lumps. Once the soup is boiling, slowly whisk in the flour mixture until it's well incorporated and the soup thickens. Add in the chicken with its juices, then the evaporated milk, and stir well.

Corn Chowder

2 qt. Water (8 c.)
1 c. Potato Flakes
(not pearls)
2 (14.5 oz.) cans
Sweet Corn, drained
2 (14.5 oz.) cans
Water Chestnuts
2 (14.5 oz.) cans
Lima Beans
2 (14.5 oz.) cans Whole
Potatoes, drained and
quartered
1 (12 oz.) can Evaporated
Milk
2 tsp. Seasoning Salt
2 tsp. Poultry Seasoning
1 Tbs. Salt
1/4 tsp. Pepper
1-2 Bay Leaves

In a large pot, bring the water to a boil. Remove from heat and add the potato flakes. Stir until they are completely dissolved. Add in the rest of the ingredients. Cook over medium heat until everything is warmed through, stirring constantly so the milk does not scorch.

Lentil Stew

1 c. Dry Lentils
1 c. Barley
2 Chicken Bouillon Cubes
1 qt. Water (4 c.)
1/2 tsp. Salt

Add everything to a medium pot, then bring to a boil. Once boiling, reduce the heat and let simmer for about 45 minutes, until the barley and lentils are soft (you may need to add a little water if it starts evaporating too much).

 This is a thick, hearty and simple stew that will keep your tummy filled for a long time.

Wheat Berry Stew

1 qt. Water (4 c.)
1 (8 oz.) can Tomato Sauce
1 (14.5 oz.) can Kidney
  Beans, drained & rinsed
1 (14.5 oz.) can Black
  Beans, drained & rinsed

1 (14.5 oz.) can Diced
  Tomatoes
1 c. Cooked Wheat Berries
1 Tbs. Taco Seasoning
1 Tbs. Seasoning Salt

Add all the ingredients to a medium pot. Bring to a boil, then simmer until everything is warmed through.

Meals

- Mashed Potato Bowls
- Spaghetti
- Red Beans and Rice
- Refried Beans and Rice
- Taco Skillet

- Skillet Enchiladas
- Hawaiian Haystacks
- Spanish Rice
- Oriental Noodles
- Chickpea Korma

When you want to sink your teeth into something comforting and delicious, these will be perfect! Get creative and start experimenting. You'd be surprised all the possibilities that open up when you know how to utilize a variety of ingredients that are shelf stable!

Mashed Potato Bowls

2 c. Potato Pearls
1 qt. Water (4 c.)
2 c. Chicken Gravy

Bring the water to a boil in a medium saucepan. Remove from the heat, then add in the potato pearls and stir well. Place the lid on, then let sit for about 5-10 minutes. Add more water if you like your potatoes thinner, or thin them out when they're done with a little water or a splash of milk.

Meanwhile, prepare your chicken gravy. Once the gravy is ready, scoop a generous portion of mashed potatoes into your bowl, then pour the gravy on top.

 This is a great recipe to add all sorts of canned vegetables to (like corn, green beans, beans, etc.). Add them to your gravy after it's cooked. Warm the gravy long enough to heat the vegetables through, then serve.

Spaghetti

1 lb. Spaghetti Noodles

1 (28 oz.) can Crushed
    Tomatoes

1 (14.5 oz.) can Diced
    Tomatoes

1 (8 oz.) can Tomato Sauce

1 (6 oz.) can Tomato Paste

1 Tbs. Basil

1 Tbs. Sugar

1 tsp. Oregano

1 1/2 tsp. Salt

Fill a large pot with enough water to boil the pasta. Bring the water to a boil, then add the pasta. Let boil for about 7-8 minutes, stirring occasionally, then strain. Run cold water over the pasta so the noodles don't stick together.

Meanwhile, prepare the sauce. In a medium saucepan, add the rest of the ingredients, then stir well. Cook over medium heat until the sauce is warmed through. Serve over the pasta.

 If you have springs of fresh basil, it can make this sauce taste even better! I also like to add a little of the pasta sauce to the noodles to keep them separated.

Red Beans and Rice

1/2 c. Water

1 tsp. Hearty Soup Blend

1 Beef Bouillon Cube

1/2 tsp. Salt

1/4 c. Water

2 Tbs. Flour

2 (14.5 oz.) cans Kidney
    Beans

2 c. Cooked Rice

In a medium saucepan, bring the water, spice blend, bouillon cube and salt to a boil. Meanwhile, mix 1/4 c. water with the flour in a small mason jar. Screw the lid on and then shake well until the flour is incorporated. Once the gravy is boiling, whisk in the flour mixture slowly. Add the beans, then cook over medium heat until the beans are warmed through.

Pour the beans over rice, or mix the beans and rice all together in a large bowl first, then serve and enjoy!

This is a great vegetarian version of a southern favorite. Typically it's spicy and has meat in it. We've made this very mild since our family doesn't like a lot of heat. If you want to jazz it up, add a few dashes of hot sauce to give it a kick.

Refried Beans and Rice

3 c. Dried Refried Beans
2 c. Water
1 tsp. Taco Seasoning
1/2 tsp. Salt

In a medium saucepan, bring the water, Taco Seasoning, and salt to a boil. Add in the refried beans, stir until covered. Remove from heat, then place the lid on and let sit for 5-10 minutes. Then remove the lid and stir.

These are thicker beans. If you prefer your beans thinner like I do, simply use 3 c. water (instead of 2 c. water), and follow the same instructions.

 These are great served with rice and some Flour or Corn Tortillas. The dried refried beans are available at LDS canneries.

Taco Skillet

1 c. Water

1 Beef Bouillon Cube

2 Tbs. Taco Seasoning

2 c. Cooked Wheat Berries

1 (14.5 oz.) can Diced
   Tomatoes

1 (14.5 oz.) can Pinto
   Beans

1 (2.25 oz.) can Olives,
   sliced

In a large skillet, bring the water and bouillon cube to a boil. Add in the rest of the ingredients and stir well. Cook over medium heat until everything is warmed through.

 This is great served with Flour Tortillas.

Skillet Enchiladas

Sauce:

1/4 c. Oil

1/4 c. Chili Powder

2 Tbs. Flour

1 (8 oz.) can Tomato Sauce

1 1/2 c. Water

1/4 tsp. Cumin

1/4 tsp. Garlic Powder

1/4 tsp. Onion Powder

1 tsp. Salt

In a large skillet over medium low heat, add the oil, chili powder, and flour. Once that is dissolved and cooked through, add in the rest of the sauce ingredients.

Stirring constantly, cook for an additional 5-8 minutes until the sauce thickens up. Reserve some sauce aside for topping your dish and for dipping your corn tortillas, if you prefer.

Filling:

2 c. Cooked Rice

1 (14.5 oz.) can Black
  Beans, rinsed and drained

1 (14.5 oz.) can Diced
  Tomatoes

1 pint jar of canned
  Chicken (with juice)

Add in the rest of the enchilada ingredients. Cook over medium heat until everything is warmed through. Serve with corn tortillas.

Hawaiian Haystacks

1 1/2 c. Long Grain Rice

1 qt. Water (4 c.)

Creamy Chicken Soup

Bring the water to a boil, then add the rice. Let boil for about 7 to 8 minutes, then remove from heat. Strain and fluff the rice. Makes about 4 cups of rice.

Pour the soup over the rice. You can top with anything you'd like or eat it plain (which is how my family prefers it).

Ideas for Toppings:
- Beans
- Chow Mien Noodles
- Corn
- Dried Fruits
- Mandarin Orange
    Slices
- Mushrooms
- Peas
- Pineapple
- Water Chestnuts, etc.

Spanish Rice

2 c. Water
1 c. Salsa
1 Chicken Bouillon Cube
1 tsp. Taco Seasoning

1 tsp. Salt
1 Tbs. Dehydrated Onion
1 1/2 c. Long Grain Rice

Bring the water to a gentle boil. Add in all the ingredients and stir well. Place the lid on your pot, then reduce the heat to low. Let cook with the lid on for about 20 minutes. Remove the lid, then stir. Makes a little over 4 cups.

 Don't scrape and stir the very bottom of the pot as there may be some rice that has stuck to the bottom.

Oriental Noodles

1 qt. Water (4 c.)
2 Chicken Bouillon Cubes
1 tsp. Garlic Powder
1/2 tsp. Onion Powder

1/4 tsp. Salt
1/4 tsp. Pepper
2 packages Ramen Noodles
(discard seasoning packets)

Bring the water and spices to a boil. Add in the noodles and let cook for about 2-3 minutes. Once the noodles are done, serve them with the broth.

 You can add anything into this simple noodle based dish. Vegetables and meats are great additions. You could also use beef bouillon instead for a different flavor.

Chickpea Korma

2 Tbs. Oil
2 Tbs. Flour
2 Tbs. Mild Curry Blend
2 tsp. Ground Coriander
2 tsp. Ground Cumin
1 tsp. Garlic Powder
1 tsp. Ground Ginger

1 tsp. Salt
1 (8 oz.) can Tomato Sauce
1 (14.5 oz.) can Coconut
   Milk
1 Chicken Bouillon Cube
2 (14.5 oz.) cans Chickpeas,
   drained and rinsed

In a medium saucepan, heat the oil over medium heat. Add the flour and spices. Cook for a few minutes until fragrant. Add in the tomato sauce and coconut milk. Crumble in the bouillon cube and bring to a boil, stirring constantly. Add the chickpeas, then reduce the heat and cook until the beans are warmed through (about 10 minutes).

If you like your sauce thinner, simply add water. This is perfect served over rice with some flour tortillas (rolled out a little thicker than usual so they resemble the traditional Indian naan bread) to use as a flat bread for mopping up all the sauce. We love Indian food and my children really enjoy kormas, which are a mild and flavorful curry.

Chapter 9

Desserts

Everyday Treats:
- Vanilla Pudding
- Chocolate Pudding
- Rice Pudding
- Apple Crisp

Special Day Treats:
- Chocolate Celebration Cake
- Thanksgiving Skillet Pie
- Christmas Cobbler
- Easter Cinnamon Roll Cake

Who doesn't like dessert?!? Just because you're going off grid doesn't mean that you can't still have a sweet treat once in a while.

Try using a muffin tin and making individual portions using a sun oven for the Special Day Treat recipes. There are many ways you can add to this list once you get the hang of baking with a cast iron skillet on a stovetop.

Vanilla Pudding

1/3 c. Sugar
3 Tbs. Cornstarch
1/4 tsp. Salt
2 1/2 c. Milk
1 Tbs. Vanilla

Combine the sugar, cornstarch, and salt together in a medium pan. Whisk in the milk, then cook over medium heat until it thickens. Once it thickens, add the vanilla.

 This is wonderful served warm over the Buttermilk Drop Biscuits with berries mixed in, or just by itself.

Chocolate Pudding

1/2 c. Sugar
3 Tbs. Cornstarch
1/4 tsp. Salt
2 Tbs. Baking Cocoa
2 1/2 c. Milk
1 tsp. Vanilla

Combine the sugar, cornstarch, salt and baking cocoa together in a medium pan. Whisk in the milk, then cook over medium heat until it thickens. Once it thickens, add the vanilla.

Rice Pudding

1 qt. Water (4 c.)
1 c. Long Grain White Rice
2 c. Coconut Cream

In a medium sauce pan, bring the water to a boil, add the rice and let boil gently for about 7-10 minutes (taste test the rice to see how long it needs to cook . . . basmati rice cooks faster than the LDS Cannery white rice). Remove from heat, strain, then fluff. Let it cool a little, then add in the coconut cream. This is a great comfort food dessert.

Chocolate Celebration Cake

1 1/2 c. Flour
1 c. Sugar
1/4 c. Baking Cocoa
1 tsp. Baking Soda
1/2 tsp. Salt
1 c. Water

1/2 c. Oil
1 tsp. Vinegar
1 tsp. Vanilla
Powdered Sugar
   (for dusting)

Heat your cast iron skillet over low heat. In a medium bowl, mix everything together well. Pour into the skillet, then cover. Let cook for 25-30 minutes, then uncovered for an additional 5-10 minutes. Remove from the heat and let cool. The top will be shiny and moist, but it will firm slightly as it cools. You can poke a toothpick through the cake to make sure it's done . . . or just sample a bite! Dust with powdered sugar and serve.

Apple Crisp

1 qt. Water (4 c.)
1 c. Brown Sugar
1 Tbs. Vanilla
1 tsp. Pumpkin Pie Spice
2 c. Dehydrated Apple
   Slices

1 1/2 c. Hot Water
1/2 c. Flour
Granola

In a medium saucepan, bring the water to a boil. Add the brown sugar, vanilla, and Pumpkin Pie Spice. Stir until the sugar is dissolved. Remove from the heat, and add the apple slices, stirring them into the liquid. Cover and let sit for 10 minutes.

Meanwhile, combine the flour and water in a mason jar. Shake until they are completely combined. Bring the apples back up to a boil on high heat. Slowly mix in the flour mixture and stir until combined. Remove from the heat. Spoon apple filling into bowls and top with granola.

 These dehydrated apple slices are from the LDS cannery. Other brands may require different cooking times.

Thanksgiving Skillet Pie

Pie Crust:
3 c. Flour
1 tsp. Salt
1/4 c. Sugar
1/4 c. Milk
1 c. Oil

In a medium bowl, combine all the ingredients. Mix together well with your hands until a dough ball forms. Press the dough by small handfuls into a cast iron skillet. Crimp the top edge and poke holes with a fork all along the bottom. Then place the skillet over low heat for 15 minutes. Meanwhile, make the filling.

Pie Filling:
1 (15 oz.) can Pumpkin Puree
1 (12 oz.) can Evaporated Milk
1 c. Sugar
2 tsp. Pumpkin Pie Spice
1/4 c. Cold Water
1/4 c. Cornstarch

In a medium saucepan, combine all the ingredients except the water and cornstarch. Heat over medium heat until it starts to slightly bubble. Combine the water and cornstarch in a mason jar, then whisk into the filling. Keep stirring until it's thick. Remove from the heat. When the crust is finished cooking, pour the pie filling into the pie crust.

Place the lid onto the skillet and let cook over low heat for 25-30 minutes. Then remove the lid and cook an additional 5 minutes. Let cool completely so it sets. This is a great pie with a tender and flaky crust!

Christmas Cobbler

1 c. Flour
1/2 c. Sugar
2 tsp. Baking Powder
1/2 c. Milk
1/4 c. Oil
1 (14.5 oz.) can Sliced Peaches (reserve the juice)

Heat your cast iron skillet over low heat. In a medium bowl, mix all the ingredients (except the peaches and their juice) together until everything is well combined. Pour into the skillet. Place the individual peach slices on the batter. Pour the juice on top, then sprinkle a light dusting of sugar over everything. Cover and let cook for 25-30 minutes, then uncovered for an additional 5 minutes.

You can use any canned fruit in this recipe. Just place the individual pieces of fruit onto the batter and pour the juice from the can on top, then sprinkle with a little sugar. All canned fruits work great for this dish!

Easter Cinnamon Roll Cake

Cake:

1 1/2 c. Flour
1/4 tsp. Salt
1/2 c. Sugar
2 tsp. Baking Powder

1 c. Milk
1/2 c. Oil
1 tsp. Vanilla

Heat your cast iron skillet over low heat. In a medium bowl, combine all the dry ingredients and mix well. Create a well in the center and add in the wet ingredients. Whisk until everything is combined and there are no lumps. Set aside.

Filling:

1/2 c. Brown Sugar
1/4 c. Oil

1 Tbs. Flour
1 1/2 tsp. Cinnamon

In a small bowl, mix all the ingredients together until there are no lumps.

Icing:

1 c. Powdered Sugar
3 Tbs. Milk
1 tsp. Vanilla

In a small bowl, combine until everything is well incorporated. Set aside.

Pour the cake into the skillet. Drop the filling in spoonfuls on top of the cake. Take a knife and gently swirl the filling into the cake. Place the lid on the skillet and let cook for 25-30 minutes, covered. Remove the lid and let cook uncovered an additional 5 minutes. Let cool, then drizzle the icing over the top by spoonfuls until it's well coated.

Chapter 10

Cleaning & Personal Care Recipes

- Laundry Detergent
- Vinegar All-Purpose Cleaner
- Tooth Powder & Face Wash
- "Poo-Free" Shampoo & Conditioner

Even if you are camping there are some comforts from home you don't want to leave behind. This small collection of recipes is easy to build off of. You can create many varieties and fragrances using essential oils or ground herbs and spices.

Laundry Detergent

1 1/2 c. Baking Soda
1 1/2 c. Washing Soda
1/2 c. Epsom Salt
2 Tbs. Salt
15 drops Peppermint Essential Oil
10 drops Lavender Essential Oil

Mix all the ingredients together well in a big bowl. Store in a mason jar. Makes about 1 qt.

How To Use:
1 c. White Vinegar
1 c. Color Safe Bleach (optional)
1 Tbs. Laundry Detergent

Use 1 Tbs. detergent per wash load, and add the vinegar for a softener (and deodorizer). The bleach works with the laundry detergent to keep your colors bright and your whites super white, but it's optional.

You can use whichever essential oils you prefer because your clothes won't smell like them. Just be sure to use something that can kill all of the funk. Citrus oils work great. Grapefruit and lemon essential oils are a yummy blend for those who do not enjoy lavender.

If you want to start using this now with your electric washer, follow the instructions above, and put the vinegar in the softener compartment and the bleach with the detergent. This works great with front-loading and top-loading washers.

Vinegar All-Purpose Cleaner

1 qt. White Vinegar (4 c.)
2 Tbs. Dried Lemon Peel

Combine the dried lemon peel with the vinegar in a mason jar. Place a cloth or wax paper between the vinegar and the lid (vinegar can corrode metal). Let this steep for at least a week. Strain out the peels and label your infused vinegar concentrate.

Add 2-4 Tbs. into a quart of water when cleaning. Put your cleaner in a spray bottle, or simply pour this into a bucket that you can dip into with a clean cloth.

Infusing your vinegar with citrus peels will kill a lot of unwanted germs, plus it smells wonderful. Orange peel works great in this recipe, too. A few drops of citrus essential oils can also work.

 You can use fresh peels, just make sure to remove them from the vinegar within one week.

Tooth Powder

In a small jar (usually a half pint jar works well), add in a good amount of baking soda. The size of jar you use will change the amount of baking soda you add in. At least 1/4 c. is a good start. Add in whatever single essential oil or blends you prefer for flavorings.

Some ideas for essential oils to use:
(Start with 1-2 drops and see how it feels on your gums and tastes, you can always add more)

- Cinnamon
- Clove
- Frankincense
- Lemon
- Myrrh
- Peppermint
- Spearmint
- Sweet Orange
- Wintergreen

 You can also use dried herbs that are finely ground instead of essential oils (like cinnamon, cardamom, thyme, etc.). Start by adding a pinch at a time, mixing it into the baking soda.

Face Wash

1 Tbs. Baking Soda

Make sure your face is damp. Mix the baking soda with enough water in your hand to make a paste. Smear it all over your face and rub gently. Rinse off and towel dry. Coconut oil or olive oil are perfect moisturizers for your face when you're finished!

"Poo-Free" Shampoo & Conditioner

"Poo-Free" refers to shampoo that does not having any sudsing commercial chemicals in it. This is a great option to have on hand.

Shampoo
2 c. Water
1 Tbs. Baking Soda

Conditioner
2 c. Water
1 Tbs. Apple Cider Vinegar

Place the ingredients for whichever product you are making into a jar and shake well. I like to use plastic squirt bottles that I can squeeze the liquid from easily.

Wet your hair well. Apply the shampoo all over the roots of your hair working it down to the ends, rubbing it in well. Rinse out thoroughly.

Follow with applying the conditioner all over your hair. Rinse out well.

Add a few drops (1-2) of essential oils to your conditioner solution to help the health of your hair. Using tea tree, rosemary, lavender or other essential oils will not only add a nice fragrance to your hair, but also help with dandruff or dry skin.

Herbal Remedies

There are a lot of herbs that I could talk about here. I have loved using herbs to help my family and friends with their ailments. However, check in the Recommended Books & Resources for more information on where to learn about herbs. I am including a few great recipes that you can make, but this is by no means all I would recommend you learn about herbs.

I will provide recipes for some very basic remedies that are simple to make. I cannot begin to teach you about all the herbal possibilities out there. All I can say is to start learning about herbs now, get good books, and let it be a spring board for you on your learning path.

Start using herbs and essential oils now! Familiarize yourself with these ideas, recipes, and treatments and apply them in your life. Try growing helpful herbs in your gardens and storing seeds. Not only would they be essential in times of need, but they can help you and your family right away with many ailments that you encounter. Plant identification is an important skill to learn, and knowing which herbs you want for which ailment will take time to learn about and experiment with.

My ideas here will be general how-to's. I will give you a few recipes that I have had great success with and some tea blends that our family loves to drink. All my recipes use dried loose herbs. If you are using fresh, then double the amount in the recipes. I have included a few recipes that use fresh ingredients (you can always experiment with dried ingredients instead for those recipes). I try to store enough of my remedies to have at least a year supply on hand for my family.

Remember that herbal recipes use "parts." This is any measurement you choose (teaspoon, tablespoon, measuring cups, spoonfuls, etc.). Just be sure to keep whatever measurement you choose consistent with the ratios in the recipes.

Consider working more with herbs, other alternative healing modalities, and essential oils on a regular basis. This will help you be more comfortable using them in times of need. You will also learn how you prefer your recipes as well. Everyone's herbal preferences are different, so try these out, see what adjustments you want to do and make them yours!

Just to be clear, I am not a doctor, nor do I make any assumptions or implications that these recipes take the place of medical treatments, prescriptions, etc. that you may be using. Always check with your doctor if you are unsure about something.

I have trained to be an herbalist (which is a fancy word for someone who has studied medicinal plants a lot, and loves to use them any chance they get).

My training has come from Rosemary Gladstar, who was trained by Juliette de Bairacli Levy, who was trained by the Gypsies and natives of the lands she traveled in the Mediterranean. I love paying tribute to those I have learned from. I get such strength from these amazing women who were pioneering herbs, living off the land, and always teaching others.

I never got a chance to meet Juliette, though her books and stories are very much in my heart. She was a true healer and loved helping others. She had a great love and reverence for the plants she used and always treated them with the utmost respect.

Rosemary is considered by many to be the mother of modern herbalism. She is as kind and gentle as the recipes she creates. I have deeply loved working with her, and learning from her in the mountains of New England, through her books, learning from her at workshops and conferences, and taking her herbalist certification course.

My mentors were folk herbalists, teaching how to use a combination of intuition and good knowledge about plants to make powerful homemade remedies. I am constantly filling Mason jar after Mason jar with herbal goodies, and continually peppering my kitchen window with concoctions that are steeping in the sunlight and the moonlight. Some remedies are potent and strong, while others are sweet and gentle, as you're about to find out in this section.

I hope these recipes inspire you to learn more about the amazing plants around you. Go on plant walks in your areas, get a book or two about herbs, and start brewing!

Herbal Remedies

- Friendship Tea
- Chocolate Mint Tea
- Breathe Better Tea
- Ginger Lemon Decoction
- Honey Cough Drops
- Ginger Lozenges
- Expectorant Cough Syrup
- Elderberry Cough Syrup
- Fire Cider
- Apple Cider Tonic
- Garlic Onion Honey or Oil
- Pain Relief Oil

These remedies really cover a lot of the basic every day ailments that you come across. Herbs can be very powerful and can help with a plethora of things. Let this chapter be a motivation for you to try your hand at making delicious and effective remedies. Hopefully it will inspire you to learn more about herbs. They really are fascinating and wonderful gifts for all of us to utilize.

Herbal Tea Method

I can only tell you my personal preference for how I like to make my herbal tea. Everyone is different, so try this and see how you would like to adjust it for your own family. I like my tea a little stronger, with a touch of sweetness.

1 qt. Water (4 c.)

1/4 c. Loose Herbs (flowers and leaves; use a tea ball if you have one or simply add them straight into the pot)

1/4 c. Sugar (or honey)

Bring the water to a boil, then take the pot off the heat. Add in the herbs, stir gently, then place the lid on the pot. Let the herbs steep for 15-30 minutes, depending on which herbs you've chosen (flowers require shorter time to steep, roots and barks are for herbal decoctions).

Strain out the herbs, then return the water to the pot. Add sugar (or honey), and place the lid back on. The tea is ready to drink.

Personally, I love a spot of cream in most of my teas. I find anything with berries in it will curdle the milk, so that has been my only exception. If you're like me and really want some cream in your tea, you can store powdered creamer, or use evaporated milk.

Herbal Decoction Method

Roots, barks, twigs, resins, seeds, needles, dried berries and other harder plant materials require a decoction. This differs from the herbal tea preparation in that you don't steep these plant parts, you simmer them.

1 qt. Water (4 c.)
1/4 c. Hard Plant Materials
Sweetener (the amount will vary depending on what plants you use)

In a medium saucepan, bring the water and plant materials to a boil. Reduce the heat, cover and simmer for 20-30 minutes. Strain out the plant materials, then add your sweetener.

Herbal Oil

Some herbs extract very well in oils. I prefer olive oil, but the shelf life isn't as long as other oils. Another one I would consider for this purpose would be coconut oil, though it would have to be warmed up and not solid if you wanted to use it in this manner. Both can penetrate the epidermal layer of the skin and get to the dermis layer, which is great for absorption.

Place your food or herbs (whether fresh or dried, make sure it's slightly chopped) into a pint-sized mason jar. Cover with oil completely to the top of the jar. Place a lid on it and let steep in the oil on the shelf for at least 1 week. Shake each day.

Strain out the food or herbs, then pour the oil into a new jar.

This is very useful rubbed onto the tops and soles of the feet, then cover with socks. It's great to do just before bedtime. This is a very effective way to get herbs into the body. It's also gentle enough to use on children.

Herbal Cough Syrup

Cough syrup is really easy and delicious to make yourself. You begin by making a very strong decoction, usually using berries and/or roots.

It's important to let your decoction reduce as it's simmering (usually about 30 minutes for 1 qt. of water) so you are left with about half the amount of water when it's finished simmering. Reducing the amount of water with the herbs helps concentrate all the medicinal goodness.

Then you simply strain your herbs out and add your sweetener (preferably honey). This will last for a long time and is a great way to get children to take their medicine.

Friendship Tea

Rosemary taught me that a great tea is measured by how many cups you go back for. If it's less than 3 cups, keep tweaking it.

- 2 parts Linden Flowers
- 1 part Peppermint
- 1 part Spearmint
- 1 part Lavender Buds
- 1 part Chamomile
- 1 part Oatstraw
- 1 part Rose Petals

Prepare using the Herbal Tea Method.

I created this to drink when friends stopped by. My trip to France was a big inspiration for all the herbs and flavors. My children and I enjoy it a lot and make it over and over again. I hope you like it too!

Chocolate Mint Tea

3 parts Peppermint
1 part Roasted Cacao Nibs

Prepare using the Herbal Tea Method.

When I was with one of my best friends, we went to this wonderful little nook that sold an array of homemade delights and they had a great herbal tea assortment. We sipped tea, nibbled on goodies, talked all evening, and had the best time together. The tea I enjoyed by the cupfuls was a beautiful mix of chocolate and mint that was from Provence, France. This tea is really close to that blend and takes me back to that fun night with my friend each time I brew up a batch.

Breathe Better Tea

- 3 parts Peppermint
- 1 part Lavender Buds
- 1 part Oatstraw
- 1 part Sage
  (not ground)
- 1 part Rosemary
  (not ground)
- 1 part Thyme
  (not ground)
- 1 part Chamomile

Prepare using the Herbal Tea Method.

I created this blend for my friend who had horrible asthma all her life. She could breathe so much better when she had this tea, and carried some with her in a thermos wherever she went after I made this blend for her. It's great if you have any respiratory troubles.

This is a more bitter tea, and one I do not recommend having with any dairy.

Ginger Lemon Decoction

1 qt. Water (4 c.)
2-3 Tbs. Ginger Root, chopped
1/2 c. Lemon Juice
1/4 c. Sugar or Honey

Bring the water and ginger to a boil, then let simmer for 20 minutes, covered. Once it's finished, strain out the ginger, then add the lemon juice and sweetener.

This is a great tea to take when you feel a sickness coming on. Ginger is one of the few things that can really stop a virus in its tracks!

Honey Cough Drops

2 c. Water
1/4 c. Breathe Better Tea
1 1/2 c. Honey

In a medium saucepan, bring the water to a boil. Remove from the heat and add the tea blend. Cover and let steep for 15 minutes. Strain the herbs out and rinse the saucepan. Pour the tea back into the saucepan and add in the honey.

Bring to a boil, then reduce the heat to a simmer. Let simmer until you've reached the "hard crack stage," which is 300 degrees Fahrenheit. You can drop a little of the mixture into cold water to test (it should crack apart when you remove it from the cold water), or have a candy thermometer to know how hard your mixture is getting.

Pour by 1/2 tsp. drops onto either parchment paper, a silicone baking mat, or silicone molds. Once dried and hard, coat with powdered sugar so they don't stick together (or you could wrap them in wax paper).

 Make these in small batches since they don't store long term very well.

Ginger Lozenges

1 c. Sugar
1/2 c. Water
2 Tbs. Lemon Juice
2 Tbs. Honey
1 Tbs. Ground Ginger

Bring all the ingredients to a boil, then reduce the heat to a simmer. Let simmer until you've reached the "hard crack stage," which is 300 degrees Fahrenheit (it should crack apart when you remove it from the cold water).

Pour by 1/2 tsp. drops onto either parchment paper, a silicone baking mat or silicone molds. Once dried and hard, coat with powdered sugar so they don't stick together (or you could wrap them in wax paper).

 Store in an air tight container. You can also add a couple of these to a hot cup of water and dissolve them for a cup of ginger tea! Make these in small batches since they don't store long term very well.

Expectorant Cough Syrup

This is used when you have something you're trying to cough up (like mucus). It's a double-reduction syrup, so it's very strong and works great!

1 part Wild Cherry Bark (I used 1/2 c.)
1/4 part Echinacea Root (I used 1/4 c.)
1/8 part Licorice Root (I used 2 Tbs.)
1/16 part Whole Cloves (I used 2 tsp.)
2/3 c. Honey (or 1 c. Sugar)

Fill a medium pot with 2 qt. water. Add in all the ingredients except the honey (or sugar). Bring to a simmer, partially uncovered, until reduced by almost half (about 30 minutes). Strain out the herbs and return the tea back to the pot. Add in the honey (or sugar) and reduce over medium heat until it has reduced by another half (another 30 minutes). Store in a mason jar.

I made this for a group of our Amish friends. Their entire community got whooping cough, and within about a week of everyone taking this by the spoonful every few hours, the whooping cough was completely gone! I made quarts and quarts of this for them, and the children loved it.

Elderberry Cough Syrup

1 c. Dried Elderberries
    (if using fresh, then double the amount)
1 qt. Water (4 c.)
2 Tbs. Dried Ginger Root (1/4 c. if using fresh, chopped)
1 tsp. Cinnamon (or 1-2 sticks)
1/2 tsp. Whole Cloves
1 c. Honey

In a medium saucepan, add in all the ingredients except the honey. Bring to a gentle simmer on low heat. Let this mixture reduce by about half, about 15-20 minutes. Strain out the herbs, and pour into a mason jar. Once cooled, add the honey, screw the lid on and shake well.

You can use any berry. Typically, dried elderberries are used, but anything with a lot of antioxidants (berries with deep color) will work fine. Rose hips, hawthorn berries, chokecherries, huckleberries, etc. This is great to take for all the vitamins and antioxidants in it, as well as warding off any colds or flus.

Rosemary's Fire Cider

1/2 c. Horse Radish (peeled and grated)
1/2 c. Garlic (peeled and chopped)
1/2 c. Onions (peeled and chopped)
1/2 c. Ginger (peeled and grated)
2 Tbs. Lemon Juice
2 Tbs. Dried Rosemary
1 Tbs. Turmeric
1/4 tsp. Cayenne Powder
Raw Apple Cider Vinegar
Honey

Place all the ingredients except the vinegar and honey into a quart-sized mason jar. Fill to the top with apple cider vinegar. Place wax paper between the lid and the vinegar, then screw the ring on (vinegar can corrode the canning lid, so the wax paper is important). Let sit on the shelf for 1 month. Shake it regularly.

Strain out the ingredients and pour the liquid into a mason jar. Add 1/4 c. honey, taste, and add a little more until it's to your desired sweetness. Don't make it too sweet . . . it's supposed to have a kick in it!

Fire cider is just that, full of fire! This is a wonderful winter tonic Rosemary Gladstar created to help ward off that bug that's usually going around. This is my twist on her classic recipe. She made it almost 50 years ago and it's still being made routinely in homes all over the world today! Take it as needed (preferably not on an empty stomach). One ounce a day (2 Tbs.) is the recommended dose for an adult to start with.

Apple Cider Tonic

1/2 c. Apple Juice
1 1/2 c. Water
1/4 c. Honey
2 Tbs. Raw Apple Cider Vinegar
1 tsp. Vanilla
1/2 tsp. Cinnamon
1/4 tsp. Turmeric
1/4 tsp. Cardamom

Put all the ingredients in a quart sized mason jar and shake well. You can drink this right away. Makes 2 cups.

I made this as a tonic to take when I started feeling that itch in the back of my throat. It's a little gritty, but really works like a charm. Just give it a quick shake or stir before you drink! This is really great when you make it with really cold water, and pour it over ice.

Garlic Honey & Garlic Oil

Garlic Honey

1 head of garlic, chopped
1 onion, chopped
Rosemary, Thyme, Sage (If fresh, use 1 good handful of each and roughly chop. If dried and not powdered, use about 1 heaping Tbs. of each)
Honey

Put all the ingredients except the honey into a pint-sized mason jar. Slowly add the honey. You may need a knife or stick to gently help any air bubbles to pop. Once everything is well covered, fill the jar to the top. Place a lid on it and let it sit on the shelf at least 1 week. Shake often. The juices from the onion and garlic will loosen up the honey. Strain out the herbs and store the infused honey in a new jar. Take by the spoonful whenever you feel like you're coming down with something.

Garlic Oil

Make the same recipe as the Garlic Honey, except use olive oil instead of honey. Use gloves and cotton balls and apply to the bottoms and tops of the feet, then put socks on before bed.

 I have had bad results when I have used commercial honey. I never have had a batch turn out bad with local raw honey. Buy your honey from a good beekeeper!

Pain Relief Oil

1/2 c. Olive Oil
2 Tbs. Powdered Cayenne

In a small saucepan, simmer 2 pints of water. Once the water is up to a simmer, place the oil and cayenne in a heat-safe bowl over top the saucepan. You will need to double boil the oil so it can infuse with the powdered cayenne. Cook gently over the low heat for about 20 minutes, then remove from heat and keep warm.

You can repeat this process by straining out the powder from the oil using a cloth. Add another 2 Tbs. of powder and double boil it another 20 minutes to increase its potency, but this is optional. Once finished, strain off the powder through a cloth again and bottle the oil.

This oil will need to be used cautiously. Make sure your hands stay clean (you don't want to get this in your eyes!). Rub it gently on sore joints and muscles many times a day for relief. Cotton balls and latex gloves work great for this!

Chapter 11

72 Hour Kit Preparation Ideas

72 hour kits are invaluable to have on hand in case of an emergency. These are kits that have enough supplies to sustain you and your family for 3 days. These can be useful for a number of emergency situations…anything from a major emergency such as a community evacuation during a natural disaster, to a minor emergency like a temporary power outage in your area. These kits are essential to maintain health, emotional stability, and also benefit others who are not as prepared.

As I have mentioned before, I am a member of The Church of Jesus Christ of Latter-day Saints. Though this book is by no means a representation of the Church's opinion, you will see some items I recommend (such as scriptures, blessings, family history, etc.) included in this list. These items are things that I cherish and are a part of my faith. I would highly suggest that you include things that are precious to you that are a part of your faith as well, whichever faith that may be. Those items will bring a lot of peace and comfort in a traumatic situation.

Listed are a few categories to think about when planning your 72 hour kit:
- Clothing
- Comfort Items
- First Aid Kit
- Food
- Sanitation
- Survival Tools

I have put together a list for each category with ideas for things that you could put into your kits. These suggestions are not "one size fits all"...be sure to customize your kits to meet your family's needs.

I hope these ideas help you to be better prepared. I have a true testimony of the peace that we can receive when we are ready for any situations that may come our way. That peace is magnified ten-fold when we are able to help others as well. It is my prayer that the spirit of preparedness can burn within you, and that you can also help those you love ignite a passion for creating their own 72 hour kits.

Clothing

I love the rule of thumb to update your 72 hour kit every 6 months (around Daylight Savings Time). It helps you pack according to the upcoming weather and it's a great calendar marker to keep it fresh and in season. Three days' worth of clothing really isn't much. I like to make sure that the items are practical, and not cumbersome in material or style.

- Baseball hats (with hair ties and hair clips for girls; they're wonderful for keeping you protected and the sun out of your eyes)
- Ponchos (these are great if it rains)
- Socks
- Sweatshirts/ Jackets (the evenings get cool even in the summer, and it's a great layer in the winter)
- Tops/ Bottoms (pack according to the weather)
- Underwear (even if you can't change your clothing, changing the under garments can make a huge difference in your hygiene and personal comfort)

Comfort Items

We all need comfort! This is, in my opinion, the funnest part of the kit to pack, especially for our children. There may be time for these items during an emergency, and there may not. They can really boost moral when spirits are low. I would suggest having extra candy & small toys (even if you don't have children) to pass out to other children to comfort them, too.

- Compact Scriptures/ Patriarchal Blessing (any other important books, papers, or quotes that can bring you comfort and peace when you are distraught)
- Games (small ones for road trips or travel games work well)
- Gum (not mint-flavored! sticks are easier and more compact to pack)
- Hard Candy (butterscotch, root beer barrels, caramels, etc.)
- Instruments (harmonica, flutes, kazoos, etc.)
- Silky/ Polyester Blankets for children
- Small Toys (cars, dolls, sticker books, figurines, etc.)
- Neck Pillows (these are tiny pillows that will make all the difference when you're resting on the ground or somewhere that has a hard surface)

First Aid Kits

It's really easy to get caught up in how much of this or that we need to have in our first aid kits...but I can't stress enough how important it is to be spiritually, mentally, and emotionally pre-pared for whatever calamities might come our way, both major and minor. That is where the real preparing needs to be happening right now, both in our homes and within ourselves. All the rest of this is superfluous without a firm foundation. I pray we're all able to keep our strength and our faith, no matter how hard the future gets.

Now please keep in mind, this is mostly going to be used for minor emergencies, and it's only for 3 days . . . it's not something that you can bug out with and live alone with for years. I am focusing on the basic needs. You could pack the kitchen sink if you feel the need, but this is just for minor emergencies. You could do the what-if's for a plethora of things that could go wrong . . . but it'll drive you crazy and you can never pack enough, or everything. So keep it simple.

I am not a nurse, nor do I plan on having to do surgery. That said, this is a basic list, so please add to it according to your skills and family needs. I hope you can take any of these suggested items and see what you need for your kits and feel better prepared for what calamities might come your way.

I would highly recommend learning Basic First Aid, CPR, and other helpful skills that could not only benefit your family, but many others. The Red Cross offers many classes that you can take and learn from. They offer extensive training in many areas, and it's easy to sign up for one class at a time, as your schedule allows.

Minor Emergency Supplies

Bites & Stings

- Bite Kit (for snake bites or other venomous bites), Lavender Essential Oil, Anti-Itch Cream
- Blisters
- Moleskin & Band Aids
- Coughs & Allergies
- Cough Drops, Allergy Medicine

Cuts & Burns

- Band-Aids (varying sizes and shapes, I like the fabric kind best)
- Bandages (especially the butterfly ones)
- Essential Oil (lavender is a great one for burns as well as bites)
- Dental Kit and Supplies (for minor dental emergencies)

Heat Stroke & Dehydration

- Water Filters
- Water
- Sunscreen
- Chapstick
- Chinese Fans, and Mini Spray Bottles to keep you cooled off

Hypothermia & Shock

- Emergency Blankets (these are thin metallic blankets used for shock or hyperthermia, they are not everyday blankets)

Pain & Headaches

- Medicine (for headaches and pain)
- Analgesic Spray

Sanitation

- Rubbing Alcohol
- Hydrogen Peroxide
- Antiseptic Spray
- Antibiotic Ointment
- Melaleuca Oil
- Gloves (there could be blood or other body fluids that you have to work with)
- Hand Sanitizer
- Antibacterial Wipes

Sprains & Strained Muscles

- Ace Bandages
- Ice & Heat Packs (they're activated when they're squeezed until you hear a click and the chemical reactions happen, and they're only good for one use and last a few hours)

Tools

- Cotton Balls, Gauze in a Roll or Package (for bigger wounds or cleaning out wounds)
- Tape (Duct Tape and Athletic Tape),
- Tweezers
- Scissors
- Safety Pins
- Bandanas (these are multi purpose, and really useful to wear on your face if the air is contaminated)
- Q-Tips, Finger Nail Clippers
- Consecrated Oil (obtained through a worthy LDS Priesthood holder)

Upset Stomach & Diarrhea

- Peppermints
- Fennel Seeds
- Ginger Chews for upset stomachs
- Pills for Diarrhea
- . . . and of course, any personal medications you are taking (including EpiPens, inhalers, insulin and diabetic supplies, or items of that nature) that you want to keep with you at all times.

Food

When planning your family's 72 hour kit, the first thing that usually comes up is, "what are we going to eat?" These ideas are meant to be a springboard for you to utilize and customize to your family's needs. As you keep tweaking what works better for your kits, they will be even more functional and practical.

I have looked for ideas all over the internet. Some are great, while others are full of Goldfish and beef jerky…for dinner! This was a big hurdle for me to tackle. What could I pack that's not junk for 3 days? I needed something that could actually sustain my family, giving us the energy we need in case we're hiking out of a natural disaster or something similar to that.

I found there were actually many ideas out there that were exactly what I was looking for, and I'm excited to share some of my ideas with you.

I can't stress this enough…test your kit out! Whether you are out camping or at home, put your kit to the test and see if it is able to take care of your family.

One key aspect to preparing your 72 hour kit, especially concerning food, is to pack extra. It's so important to pack extra items that you can share with others who are traumatized and are not prepared. Helping others is a wonderful way to relieve stress and the emotional turmoil that you may be experiencing. Whenever you give service, it brings you out of your own perspective and strengthens the hope that you will be okay.

Breakfast Ideas

Be sure to start your day off with the feeling that "you've got this," that you're prepared, and that your family can handle anything you come across! If you are using your kit, chances are you are being plucked from all the comforts of your home and roughing it somewhere. Make sure you feel like your family is ready to start your day off with good spirits and happy tummies!

- Canned Fruit (you can eat right out of the can, and it's a great filler)
- Cold Cereal (I like my Granola from the breakfast section; you can eat it dry and drink your juice)
- Granola Bars (I really like the basic crunchy ones, made of oats…they don't have as many candy add-ins and they don't melt)
- Juice (it's important to get your blood sugar going in the morning)

Lunch Ideas

I am not a huge fan of making a big lunch. I tend to focus more on dinner, so this list is going to be more "snacky." Avoid things with too much salt, since it will make you thirsty. Beef jerky is a really popular item in 72 hour kits, but unless you remember to pack floss and have lots and lots of water, it's not something I'd recommend. Keep in mind that while hiking, you probably won't want to stop and have a long lunch. These items may be eaten in spurts throughout your day until evening.

- Cans of V8
- Cheese and Cracker combo packs
- Dried Fruit (raisins, craisins, apricots, etc.)
- Energy Bars (these are great for the calories, keep your blood sugar up, easy to hand out to others, plus they don't require cooking)
- Fruit Snacks or Fruit Leather (get real stuff, not the fake stuff)
- Gatorade, or something like it (by lunch time your body will be really tired, and you've probably been sweating a lot if you're hiking, so make sure your electrolyte levels are happy)
- Packages of Peanut Butter and Crackers
- Trail Mix
- Water

Dinner Ideas

So you've had a long hard day, you're a little traumatized, and you all just want to sit and never get up again! Make sure that dinner is comforting, it's warm (if you have the ability to cook it), and can help you have a good night's sleep. You're going to be away from your bed and all that you've ever known, so be sensitive to that. Be sure that everyone is full and their spirits are up so you can all sleep well. Making sure your food is yummy is a big help in this situation!

- Anything left over from the other meals!!!
- Canned Meat (beef, chicken, spam, corned beef, beef stew, soups, etc.)
- Canned Veggies (anything that be drained and eaten

right out of the can such as corn, carrots, green beans, garbanzo beans, butter beans, etc.)
- Chicken Salad with Cracker packages
- "Just Add Water" soup mixes (soup can be thinned out to feed more people, and they can also be eaten warm or cold)
- Pouches of "Just Add Water" foods (instant potatoes, soups, pasta, etc.)
- Pureed Fruit Pouches (like applesauce)
- Water

Snacks

Well yes, you will need snacks! I'm not referring to cookies and milk (though that would be awe-some). I am more referring to candy. It keeps your sugar levels good, keeps everyone happy, and keeps your mouth from drying out. Hard candies are best because they don't melt and they don't make a mess. I would stay away from suckers as you don't want any accidents, like running with a stick in your mouth and stuff . . . it happens. Including gum in your kit will help your ears pop if you're moving to higher elevations as well.

- Butterscotch
- Chocolate-Flavored Hard Candies
- Gum (not mint-flavored! . . . it will make everything taste like mint in your kits)
- Hard Caramels
- Jolly Ranchers
- Peppermints (great if you can't brush your teeth, and for upset stomachs)
- Root Beer Barrels
- Tootsie Rolls

Sanitation

This is such a huge topic, because if you don't keep everything clean, you're in for a mess of problems (wasn't that a great pun?!?) . . . okay, I've been talking about this for too long!

Seriously though, I have been through a major catastrophe in a freak snow storm that cut our power for weeks when we first moved to New York. Everything that could go wrong did! One of the biggest problems we experienced was sanitation. I've compiled a list of a few items that are excellent to have on hand when everything is upside-down in your life.

These items will take up the least amount of space if you take everything out of their boxes and packages and store them in Ziploc bags.

Body Fluids

We're not used to roughing it completely yet, so make sure to have some toilet paper! It's easier to store if you take the roll out and put it in a quart-sized Ziploc bag. Also, remember items that you need for your family members such as diapers, pull-ups, extra underwear, etc., and wipes for any cleaning up you may have to do.

Dirt

Soap!!! This is something that's worth its weight in gold! Have plenty of those small travel-sized soap bars.

Wet/ Dry Items

• Grocery Bags
• Trash Bags

- Ziploc Bags (these are great to keep soiled clothing in, to keep things dry and separate, like your toothbrush and numerous other things)

Feminine Issues

- Feminine Products (along with extra underwear)

Hygiene

- Toothbrushes
- Toothpaste
- Brushes, Combs
- Hair Ties
- Contact Solution
- Shampoo
- Conditioner
- Soap
- Wash Cloths
- Deodorant
- Q-Tips
- Fabric
- Perineal Bottles
- Lotion

Wounds

- Wipes
- First Aid Kit
- Consecrated Oil
- Hand Sanitizer

Survival Tools

These are general items that could come in handy for many situations. There are too many what-if situations to list, so just keep in mind that these items could double and be used for numerous circumstances. These items can help us get to a safe place and keep us supplied with the things we may need for 3 days.

- Axe/ Saw/ Shovel
- Candles
- Can Opener
- Compact Sewing Kit
- Compass
- Cooking Items and Tools (compact burner, small pot, etc.)
- Duct Tape
- Emergency Kit for your vehicle (make sure it has flares, cables, lights, emergency blankets, water, hard candy, coloring books and things for kids, tire patch kit, tire pressure kit, spare tire, money, gas can (or sterilized milk jug), chapstick, and separate mini first aid kit that is just used for and kept in the car)
- Field Guides (especially 4-season ones for your area: trees, plants, flowers, mushrooms, etc.)
- Flares
- Flashlights (extra batteries in a Ziploc bag)
- Fishing Line (hooks)
- Gloves (leather or gardening)
- Important Documents (even if they are just copies, keep them in a flexible binder with page protectors)
- Maps (local maps)
- Matches & Lighter (in a Ziploc bag)
- Mess Kit

- Money & Change (in small bills, in a Ziploc bag)
- Mirror (at least the size of your hand, so you can signal with it)
- Multivitamins & Minerals
- Paper & Pens (in a Ziploc bag)
- Pet Care Supplies (if applicable)
- Pocket Knives (Leatherman, Gerber for additional tools)
- Radio (extra batteries in a Ziploc bag)
- Rope
- Sleeping Bags
- Tarp
- Tent
- Watch
- Water Purification Tablets
- Whistle
- Zip Ties

This concludes my list of 72 hour kit ideas! I would really suggest practicing with your family. Make sure your bag or whatever you're carrying is right for you and each member of your family. Test your preparations, go camping, and see how you do. Having functional 72 hour kits will bring you a lot of peace of mind, as well as relief, if any calamity were to occur. Good luck with all your preparations!

Ideas For Long Term Camping Supplies

This list is by no means a comprehensive list...it's simply for stimulating ideas of things to consider when preparing for your family's needs in a long-term camping situation. These items listed below would be in varying amounts, depending on your family's needs. See the 72 Hour Kit section for an itemized list of similar items, but keep in mind that not everything listed here would necessarily pertain to a 72 Hour Kit, and vice versa.

- Batteries (with Solar Charger)
- Bandages (Ace Wraps, Band-Aids, Gauze Pads, etc.)
- Binoculars (small and large)
- Birthing Kit (Bulb Syringes, Cord Clamps, Gloves, Newborn Diapers, Onsies, Perineal Bottles, Receiving Blankets, Scissors, etc.)
- Books (Field Guides, Health, Personal Reading, Skills, Spiritual, Reference, etc.)
- Broom & Dustpan (the small hand held ones, to clean your tent)
- Camping Cookbooks (this book as well as others for dutch oven cooking, and more are very useful)
- Camping Equipment (Tarps, Tents, Wood Stoves, etc.)
- Canning Supplies (Jars, Lids, Pectin, Pots, Tools, etc.)
- Cleaners (Bleach, Vinegar, etc.)
- Clothing (for all seasons, Coats, Hats, Shawls, Wool Socks, etc.)
- Comfort Items (Blankets & Toys for Children, Classic Story Books, Games, etc.)
- Compass
- Contact Solution (Eye Drops for itchy eyes)

- Cooking Supplies (listed in the Recommended Tools section)
- Cotton Swabs (Cotton Balls & Q-Tips)
- Craft Supplies (Crocheting, Beading, Boondoggle, Embroidery, Knitting, Sewing, etc.)
- Dental Kit (Basic Dental Tools, Cotton Pads, Floss, Tooth Repair Products, etc.)
- Essential Oils (with reference materials)
- Eye Glasses (a few backup pairs for everyone in your family who needs them & Sunglasses)
- Family History (Charts, Photobooks, Stories, Thumb Drives with Pictures & Video on them, etc.)
- First Aid Kit (Anti-Itch Creams, Bandanas, Hot Water Bottles, Hydrogen Peroxide, Melatonin, Rubbing Alcohol, Tools, etc.)
- Flashlights & Lanterns (solar if possible)
- Gardening Supplies (Gloves, Seeds, Tools, etc.)
- Hair Supplies (Bobbie Pins, Brushes, Clips, Combs, Hair Ties, Headbands, Ribbons, etc.)
- Hygienic Supplies (Deodorant, Feminine Supplies, Fabric, Floss, Perineal Bottles, Razors, Toilet Paper, Toothbrushes, etc.)
- Instruments (Harmonicas, Kazoo, Flutes, Ukulele, etc.)
- Multi-Vitamins & Minerals
- Personal Care Tools (Nail Clippers, Mirror, Razors, Tweezers, etc.)
- Pictures (laminated pictures of religious leaders, family, and others that you want to reference)
- Radios (Ham, Solar, etc.)
- Sentimental Items (Letters, Jewelry, Trinkets, etc.)
- Scissors (different kinds for cutting hair, fabric, thicker material, etc.)
- Shoes (closed toe for all seasons)

- Skills (Cutting Hair, Fishing, Healing Arts, Hunting, Sewing, Tai Chi, Yoga, etc.)
- Skin Care (Creams, Lotions, Oils, Scrubs, Sunblock, etc.)
- Sleeping Gear (Cots, Blankets, Sleeping Bags, Sleeping Bag Liners, Pillows, etc.)
- Soap (Bar, Dish, Hand, Laundry, Shampoo & Conditioner, etc.)
- Spiritual Prep Kit (Journal & Writing Tools, Magazines, Pictures, Stories, Talks, etc.)
- Survival Gear (Compass, Fishing Supplies, Gloves, Hunting Supplies, Pantyhose, Zip Ties, etc.)
- Tool Kit (Duct Tape, Gloves, Tape, Hammer, Nails, Rope, Saw, Shovel, etc.)
- Towels & Washcloths
- Transportation (Bicycles, Carts, etc.)
- Washing Supplies (Basins, Bowls, Buckets, Washboards)
- Whistles
- Writing Supplies (Construction Paper, Crayons, Notebooks, Paper, Pens, Pencils, Sharpeners, etc.)

Tips Shared By Long Term Campers

- Get used to dirt, it's on everything, and will always be everywhere.
- Make peace with the spiders—they eat mosquitoes!
- Raccoons have no respect for personal property.
- Make peace with skunks . . . or your life will stink.
- Know your plants, the good, the bad, and the pokey!
- Always look where you decide to answer nature's call, at least 3 times!
- Don't camp by still water.
- Clear the area well before you tie down your tent (no rocks, roots, etc.).
- Shake your clothes really well each day before putting them on!
- Always, ALWAYS check your shoes before putting them on.
- Change out of day clothes each night, damp ones will make you colder.
- Always zip your tent closed at night.
- Keep a small flashlight under your pillow for night time bathroom trips.
- Duct Tape is more valuable than gold when camping, always have it!
- A tent with a floor is better than not, but it still needs a ground cover.
- Take care of your feet, use foot powder, change your socks, etc.
- Personal hygiene is key, keep clean, especially small scrapes and cuts.
- Embrace the art of improvising, you'll never be able to pack everything!

- The stars are beautiful, don't ignore them!
- Kids won't be bored, they'll always find things to play with for hours!
- Start bird watching, enjoy the species that live around you.
- Never eat anything if you don't know what it is.
- Learn which foods you can forage, it's a lot of fun to do with kids!
- Get to know mushrooms, fishing, plants, constellations, animal tracks, etc.
- Sing songs a lot, it makes for a much happier camper, try it!
- You really don't need as much stuff as you think, the basics are enough.
- No matter what's for dinner it's going to taste great after a long hard day.
- Get comfortable with uncomfortable, yes it's going to be different now.
- Get used to the sounds of nature . . . especially at bedtime.
- Respect the wilderness, keep it clean and it will respect you.
- Share the little things, they're really the big things all added up.
- Trust more, there is no book to double-check, trust yourself & trust the Lord!

Chapter 12

Complete List Of Items Used In This Book

Every Item Listed In The Recipe Sections

Baking Items

- Baking Cocoa
- Baking Powder
- Baking Soda
- Brown Sugar
- Cornstarch
- Honey
- Lemon Juice
- Maple Extract
- Olive Oil
- Powdered Sugar
- Salt
- Sugar
- Vanilla Extract
- Vegetable Oil
- Vinegar (White & Apple Cider)

Canned Items

- Black Beans
- Black Olives
- Coconut Milk
- Chicken
- Chickpeas (Garbanzo Beans)
- Corn
- Crushed Tomatoes (28 oz.)
- Dehydrated Apple Slices
- Diced Tomatoes
- Evaporated Milk
- Great Northern Beans
- Kidney Beans
- Lima Beans
- Mandarin Oranges
- Mushrooms
- Peaches
- Pineapple
- Pinto Beans
- Potatoes (whole or quartered)
- Pumpkin
- Salsa
- Tomato Paste
- Tomato Sauce (8 oz.)
- Water Chestnuts

Drinks

- Cocoa Mix
- Fruit Drink Mix
- Powdered Milk
- Water

Dry Beans & Legumes

- Black Beans
- Dehydrated Refried Beans
- Great Northern Beans
- Green Lentils
- Kidney Beans
- Pinto Beans
- Red Lentils
- Split Green Peas

Dry Spices

- Basil
- Bay Leaves
- Beef Bouillon Cubes
- Cardamom Pods (green)
- Celery Salt
- Cinnamon (ground)
- Cinnamon Sticks
- Cloves (ground)
- Cloves (whole)
- Coriander
- Chicken Bouillon Cubes
- Chili Powder
- Cumin
- Dehydrated Onions
- Fennel Seed (ground)
- Garlic Powder
- Ginger (ground)
- Lavender
- Marjoram
- Nutmeg
- Onion Powder

- Oregano
- Paprika
- Parsley
- Pepper (ground)
- Peppercorns
- Rosemary
- Sage
- Savory
- Thyme
- Turmeric

Grains & Flours

- All-Purpose Flour
- Barley
- Couscous
- Cream of Wheat
- Corn Masa Flour
- Cornmeal
- Rice (white, long-grain)
- Rolled Oats (old fashioned)
- Spelt
- Wheat Berries
- Whole Wheat Flour

Miscellaneous

- Chow Mein Noodles
- Potato Flakes
- Potato Pearls
- Ramen Noodles
- Spaghetti Noodles

Suggested Canned, Bottled, and Packaged Items

These items are not listed in any of my recipes, but they may come in handy for your planning purposes. These items are excellent resources to add to your meals. This is just a brief list of ideas, so keep adding to it and make it customized to your family's needs and preferences.

- Applesauce
- Apple Juice
- Bacon Bits
- Beans (Baked Beans, Butter, Fava, White, etc.)
- Beets (regular and pickled)
- Crackers (Animal, Graham, Triscuit, Wheat Thins, etc.)
- Condiments (Dressings, Ketchup, Mayonnaise, Miracle Whip, Mustard, Relish, etc.)
- Fish (Salmon, Sardines, Kippers, Mackerel, Tuna, etc.)
- Fruit- Dry (Raisins, Apricots, Prunes, Berries, Craisins, Candied Fruit, etc.)
- Fruit- Canned (Berries, Fruit Cocktail, Pears, Mango Slices, Mandarin Oranges, etc.)
- Garlic (picked or packed in oil)
- Green Beans
- Green Olives
- Ghee
- Grape Juice
- Gum (not mint flavored, it makes everything taste like mint)
- Hard Candy (Butterscotch, Dum-Dum Suckers, Jolly Ranchers, Peppermints, Root Beer Barrels, etc.)
- Peanut Butter
- Pickles (Bread and Butter, Dill, Sweet, etc.)
- Pickled Eggs

- Pretzels
- Sauces (BBQ, Dipping Sauces, Marinades, Steak Sauce, etc.)
- Sauerkraut
- Seasonings (any blends you enjoy and purchase all the time)
- Tomato Juice (like V-8)

Every Item Listed In The Cleaning Recipes Section

- Apple Cider Vinegar
- Baking Soda
- Epsom Salt
- Dried Lemon Peel
- Essential Oils (Citrus, Lavender, Peppermint, etc.)
- Salt
- Washing Soda
- Vinegar

Every Item Listed In The Herbal Remedies Section

- Apple Juice
- Apple Cider Vinegar
- Cardamom Pods (green)
- Cayenne Powder
- Chamomile
- Cinnamon Sticks
- Cloves (whole)
- Dehydrated Onions
- Echinacea Root
- Elderberries
- Garlic
- Ginger (ground)
- Ginger Root (dried)
- Honey
- Horseradish
- Lavender
- Lemon Juice
- Linden Flowers
- Oatstraw
- Olive Oil (extra virgin)
- Peppermint
- Roasted Cacao Nibs
- Rose Petals
- Rosemary
- Sage
- Spearmint
- Turmeric (ground)
- Wild Cherry Bark

4

Recommended Books & Resources

Cookbooks

- *It's In The Bag: A New Approach To Food Storage* by Michelle Snow
- *100 Day Pantry: 100 Quick and Easy Gourmet Meals* by Jan Jackson
- *Pantry Cooking: Unlocking Your Pantry's Potential* by Cheryl F. Driggs

Preparedness Planning

- www.beprepared.com
- www.foodstoragemadeeasy.net
- *Simply Prepared: A Guide to Emergency Preparedness and Food Storage* by Cheryl F. Driggs

Herbal Resources

- Any books written by Juliette de Bairacli Levy
- Any books written by Rosemary Gladstar, especially her latest one, *Rosemary Gladstar's Medicinal Herbs: A Beginner's Guide to Know, Grow, and Use*
- *Botany In A Day* by Thomas J. Elpel (the revised 2013 edition printed in color)
- Local Field Guides (plants, trees, mushrooms, etc.) Try to get four-season ones if you can
- For Bulk Herbs & Spices (local health food stores, Co-ops, there are also many online distributors)
- For Herbal Identification Skills (find local plant walks Google for any herbalists and nature lovers in your area)

- For Essential Oils (there are a plethora of great brands to choose from, just make sure they're pure)
- www.herbmentor.com (a great website to start learning about herbs)

LDS Church Affiliated Websites and Resources for More Information about Preparedness
- www.lds.org
- www.providentliving.org
- LDS Canneries (find one in your area)
- LDS Scriptures (which includes the King James Bible, Book of Mormon, Doctrine & Covenants, and Pearl of Great Price)

Additional Reading

- *Daughters In My Kingdom* by The Church of Jesus Christ of Latter-day Saints
- *Essentials of Home Production and Storage* by The Church of Jesus Christ of Latter-day Saints
- *Prophetic Statements on Food Storage for Latter-day Saints* by Neil H. Leah
- *Recollections of the Handcart Pioneer of 1860 (Second Edition): A Woman's Life on the Mormon Frontier* by Mary Ann Hafen
- *Tell My Story, Too—A Collection of Biographical Sketches of Pioneers and Rescuers of the Willie, Martin, Hodgett, Hunt Companies 1856* by Jolene S. Allphin
- *The Price We Paid: The Extraordinary Story of the Willie and Martin Handcart Pioneers* by Andrew D. Olsen

Chapter 13

Endure To The End

Complaining is something we're all capable of, even the best of us. Yes, we all will miss the comforts we're used to having. After about a week of camping, you're ready to run back to your warm automatic showers, soft mattresses, and speedy electric ovens. But if you can get past that, if you can see what you're doing is part of something bigger and greater, then you're going to make it. It's easy to lose sight of your goals when you can't see the end is near.

I know as we strive to obey the Prophet's council, that we will be blessed. I know that as we do our part to not only establish our food storage, but really live off it, share it, and continue to maintain it, we will have strength and a closeness to our Savior that will give vital nourishment to our spirits as well as our bodies.

When there is a will, there is a way . . . as I have been more determined to obtain our family's food storage and collect recipes that we enjoy, I have gained a greater peace of mind that we will be taken care of and have security. There is always safety in following the Lord. Cooking food storage meals that are yummy isn't always easy. I take a lot of courage from our amazing pioneer heritage. They had to eat what they had and be grateful for the most meager of meals.

Here are some quotes I've loved about enduring to the end. May this give you strength and help you on the days when you don't want to do it all again. May you feel sustained and keep on going. Your family, friends, and you will depend on it.

Quotes & Scriptures

Quotes

"Come What May, and Love It!"
— Joseph B. Wirthlin

"Often we do not know what we can endure until after a trial of our faith. We are also taught by the Lord that we will never be tested beyond that which we can endure."
— Robert D. Hales

"The blessings that come to you from enduring to the end in this life are real and very significant, and for the life to come they are beyond our comprehension."
— Dieter F. Uchtdorf

"Your responsibility to endure is uniquely yours. But you are never alone. I testify that the lifting powers of the Lord can be yours if you will "come unto Christ" and "be perfected in him.""
— Russell M. Nelson

"I am asking you to not give up "for ye are the foundation of a great work." That "great work" is you—your life, your future, the very fulfillment of your dreams. That "great work" is what, with effort and patience and God's help, you can become. When days are difficult or problems seem unending, I plead with you to stay in the harness and keep pulling. You are entitled to "eat the good of the land of Zion in these last days," but it will require your heart and a willing mind. It will require that you stay at your post and keep trying."
— Jeffrey R. Holland

"As you build your lives in obedience to the gospel and strive to achieve your goals, do not become discouraged by temporal setbacks and disappointments. Remember that 'it must needs be, that there is an opposition in all things.' You will grow and learn by overcoming obstacles. The Lord has admonished all of us to 'keep His commandments and endure to the end.'"

— Joseph B. Wirthlin

"Here then is a great truth. In the pain, the agony, and the heroic endeavors of life, we pass through a refiner's fire, and the insignificant and the unimportant in our lives can melt away like dross and make our faith bright, intact, and strong."

— James E. Faust

"I have absolute certain knowledge . . . perfect knowledge, that God loves us. He is good, He is our father, and He expects us to pray, and trust, and be believing. And not give up, and not panic, and not retreat, and not jump ship when something doesn't seem to be going just right. We stay in, we keep working, we keep believing, we keep trusting, following that same path. And we will live to fall in his arms, and feel his embrace, and hear him say, I told you it'd be okay, I told you it'd be alright."

— Jeffrey R. Holland

Scriptures

"My son, peace be unto thy soul; thine adversity and thine afflictions shall be but a small moment;

And then, if thou endure it well, God shall exalt thee on high; thou shalt triumph over all thy foes."
— D&C 121: 7-8

"Organize yourselves; prepare every needful thing, and establish a house, even a house of prayer, a house of fasting, a house of faith, a house of learning, a house of glory, a house of order, a house of God;"
— D&C 109: 8

"We glory in tribulations also: knowing that tribulation worketh patience; And patience, experience; and experience, hope: And hope maketh not ashamed; because the love of God is shed abroad in our hearts by the Holy Ghost which is given unto us."
— Romans 5: 3-5

"For after much tribulation, as I have said unto you in a former commandment, cometh the blessing. Behold, this is the blessing which I have promised after your tribulations, and the tribulations of your brethren—your redemption, and the redemption of your brethren, even their restoration to the land of Zion, to be established, no more to be thrown down."
— D&C 103: 12-13

Chapter 14

My Testimony

I have been a member of The Church of Jesus Christ of Latter-day Saints all my life. I love the gospel of Jesus Christ with everything I am made of!

I have forged a strong testimony during many small quiet moments, those moments where no one is aware but you and the Lord. The times when your integrity is tested, when character is built, and when your thoughts, motivations and actions reveal who you really are. Those are the times we find what we're truly made of.

My greatest desire is to be an instrument for the light of Christ. I am so amazed at the amount of love the Lord has for each of us. My love for the Savior has increased the closer I come to Him. My prayers are more tender, my thoughts are more focused, my motivation is to do His will not mine, and my actions have become more selfless while sincerely serving others.

I know that our Heavenly Father is aware of us and is eager to bless us. I know this through the countless times He has intervened in my life. I have had the Holy Ghost bear witness to me time after time that it was providence and His grace that was the root of my experiences. I have felt the amazing tingles of truth from my toes to the top of my head. The Spirit has born witness to me over and over of the sacred truths revealed in the Holy Scriptures, of Joseph Smith's divine mission, and of our current leaders, amazing callings to be instruments of the Lord.

I know that I am a daughter of a Heavenly Father who is

eager to see all of us return to Him, to be happy, and to share our love with others. It is my humble prayer that I can live worthy enough to have His approval and to live up to the potential that He sees in me. I pray we can all feel His love for us, even in times of uncertainty. He is with us and will never abandon us. I look forward to the day when we will shout Hosanna when He comes again, and will strive to endure until that glorious day when He will return.

In the name of my loving Savior, Jesus Christ, Amen.

About The Author

Ashley is a Texan, so her love of southern cobbler, biscuits, and beans are shared throughout this book! She started getting passionate about shelf stable cooking after she was married and started having little ones.

Ashley is a graduate from Utah State University. She lives on a hobby farm in upstate New York with her husband of 14 years and their four daughters. They stay busy beekeeping, gardening, raising lambs and chickens, and taking care of their apple orchard. She enjoys homeschooling their four girls, reading books, drawing and painting, camping, learning about biblical and LDS church history, hiking, researching her family history and doing genealogy work, watching nature shows or historic documentaries, and going on family walks.

Ashley is a Foot Zone Therapist, an herbalist, and a Tai Chi instructor. She is continually learning about energy healing and has a growing practice where she offers energy sessions, Tai Chi classes, and teaches herbal remedy courses as well.

These recipes are my gift to you. If I could, I would have you all stop by and drink a cup of tea, whip up a delicious meal with me, and enjoy a dessert together . . . this book will have to be the next best thing. I hope you share these dishes and treasures with others, and enjoy passing on the passion for delicious shelf stable cooking with those you love.

If you have any questions and want to get in touch with me about this book, or would like any additional information about energy healing, please contact me through my website at: **www.withpureintent.com**